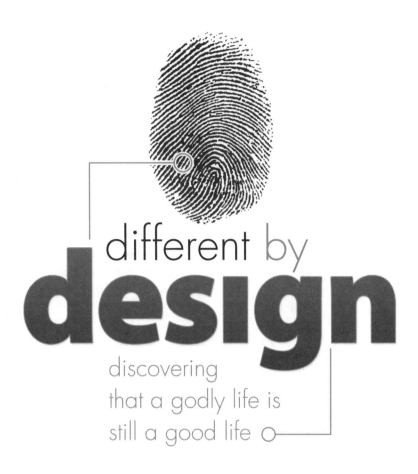

different by
design

discovering
that a godly life is
still a good life

caryschmidt

First published in 2008 by Striving Together Publications, a ministry of Lancaster Baptist Church, Lancaster, CA 93535. Striving Together Publications is committed to providing tried, trusted, and proven books that will further equip local churches to carry out the Great Commission. Your comments and suggestions are valued.

Striving Together Publications
4020 E. Lancaster Blvd.
Lancaster, CA 93535
800.201.7748

Cover design by Andrew Jones
Layout by Craig Parker
Edited by Amanda Michael
Special thanks to our proofreaders.

ISBN 978-1-59894-043-5

Printed in the United States of America

Dedication

I would like to dedicate this study to two groups of very special people:

First, to my own children—Lance, Larry, and Haylee. Bringing you up in the nurture and admonition of the Lord has been a life purpose for me and your mom. We love you beyond words; we are grateful for your tender hearts; and we long to see you embrace a godly life as you become adults and start families of your own!

Second, to the young adults of Lancaster Baptist Church with whom we are so blessed and privileged to minister. Watching your families grow in God's grace is a treasure that our hearts will never get over! We delight to see you walking in truth and living to please God in your lifestyle! Thank you for sharing your lives with our family.

Table of Contents

Acknowledgements

A project like this is the collective effort of so many wonderful and encouraging people! I am quite certain that I am blessed to work with the greatest team on the face of this planet. First, I want to thank my wife Dana for being such an amazing Christian, wife, mother, and ministry servant. Thank you for sharing these values and for helping me to transfer them to others.

I want to thank Pastor Paul Chappell for being my pastor and a tremendous spiritual undershepherd to my family. Thank you for allowing me to serve in this wonderful ministry. Special thanks to Amanda Michael and Sarah Michael for their editing, proofing, and research efforts—especially on the rules of etiquette section of this study.

Thank you to Andrew Jones for a beautiful cover design, to Craig Parker for his hard work and expertise on the layout, and to a large team of volunteer proofreaders who are not only exceptional at their work—they were extremely encouraging in the process.

It is a true privilege to work and serve with this incredible team of godly servants! They certainly model in a wonderful way the principles that are shared in this study.

Introduction
The Christian Life—**Being** or **Doing**?

A Christian friend recently made an interesting statement to me—"The Christian life is about 'being' not about 'doing.'" And honestly, at first, that statement sounded pretty solid! But the more I got to thinking about it, the more I realized there's something terribly wrong with that statement. It sounds noble. It sounds very spiritual. It even gives me a surface excuse for not *doing* some things, so long as I am *being* some things.

In other words, if you're looking for a reason not to do something that God has commanded, then this statement is perfect for you. I could reason away just about any desire of God with this statement. I could piously snub my nose at your spiritual acts of service and say, "Well, I'm more focused on *being* who God wants me to be on the inside, than merely *doing* things for God on the outside."

So, as we begin this study, I ask you to consider this question. Is the Christian life about *being* or is it about *doing*? If you look in the Bible from cover to cover, you will only come up with one answer. It is about *both*! The Bible is filled with descriptive verses about who we should be on the inside, and it's also filled with clear commands of things that we should do in our lifestyle. From page to page it describes a God who desires to transform us on the inside so that we will do His will on the outside.

If you know God at all then you know that the same God who said "the Lord looketh on the heart" also said "thou shalt not…." The same God who wants you to *be* something very specific on the inside, also expects you to *do* some very specific things in your lifestyle.

Yet we live in a day when Christians seem to want to reason away any "undesirable" lifestyle expectation of God. In other words, anything that God commands or instructs in Scripture that requires us to change our lifestyle or our behavior is being reasoned away under the guise of grace! The thought process goes something like this, "God doesn't care what I do, how I live, how I behave, or how I appear, so long as my heart is right on the inside! He's only concerned with my *being* someone for Him. He's not concerned with the things I *do*."

Friend, this thinking is terribly flawed! If you desire to know the God of the Bible and to please Him with your life, you're going to have to be concerned with both your heart *with* Him and your lifestyle *before* Him! Both matter! Both are important to God!

To be sure, God is *first* concerned with our hearts. He is *first* concerned that we are right with Him on the inside. But He is very clear in Scripture that a right heart will not be hidden! It will show up in our lifestyle. A right heart will produce a godly lifestyle. It's that simple.

God is very interested in your behavior. His desires— as expressed in His Word—are very specific regarding our outward lifestyle, but He makes it clear in Scripture that He wants a Christ-like lifestyle to flow from a Christ-like heart. He is *first* concerned with our being, but this is not His *only* concern. To say that the Christian life is about *being* is correct. But that's only half the story. The Christian life is about *being* right on the inside, and *doing* right on the outside! The two go together and are inseparable!

It's amazing how modern Christendom has reasoned such a dramatic separation between the condition of the heart and the behavior of the life. You cannot separate who you are from how you behave. One flows from the other! While it is possible, at least temporarily, to "fake" behavior and to manufacture a surface spirituality that appears to be right, it is not possible to hide a right heart. A right heart will always find it's way to the surface! It will always be seen in a right life.

Every day of your life you make judgment calls about people. You discern who they are, what they are up to, and the condition of their lives. And you make those judgment calls based upon one thing—what you see. In other words, all you can see is the lifestyle—the outward behavior. It's all that we have to work with as human beings. We can't see each other's hearts, so we generally conclude that the outward lifestyle is a pretty good reflection of the heart. And indeed it is! For when your heart is right, your life will show it clearly!

So don't fall for the "I'm all about *being* not *doing*" brand of Christianity! While it sounds good on the surface, it basically ignores about 50% of God's teachings!

I warn you, the pages you are about to read are not for the faint hearted. This book is unlike any you have probably ever read. In fact, it's not really a book. It's a study. It's a journey that will expose the terrible flawed thinking that has crept into modern Christianity. Chapter by chapter, these pages will show you a God who expects your heart for Him to show up clearly and distinctly in your lifestyle.

If you read and study these pages with an open heart, you will discover that God desires for you to make some changes. You will discover what He says about a godly lifestyle. This will not be an easy study that makes you feel warm and fuzzy on the inside while letting your lifestyle remain unchanged. Each and every page of this study will compel you to "walk worthy"—to live in a way that outwardly honors the Lord.

Living Godly Doesn't Mean You Lose Your Individuality

Perhaps our biggest threat to studying and accepting what the Word of God says about our lifestyle is that we fear losing our "individuality." So often we view our dress, our music, our hairstyles, and our mannerisms as central to who we really are—our core identities. Thus, if I have to conform or change my lifestyle for God, then I must be losing my individuality and my uniqueness. Sometimes young people call this "being crammed into a mold." We say things like, "I just don't fit that mold," and we view a godly lifestyle as something to be escaped rather than embraced.

May I challenge your thinking on this for a moment? First of all, God isn't trying to "cram you into a mold." Believe me, if He had wanted to do that, He wouldn't have made you distinctly unique to begin with! If He wanted you crammed into a mold, He wouldn't have to cram. He would only have to speak the words. God can do anything. Making you fit some preset mold would be small stuff for Him.

No, God made you unique on purpose! There is only one you! In His eternal plan, nobody else can be you, and you cannot be anybody else. You are absolutely one of a kind, and God made you specifically different by design!

Get this straight. Living for God is about being transformed and conformed to the image of Jesus Christ. And contrary to popular opinion, the more you become like Christ, the more you are *uniquely you* in God's plan! Becoming like Christ in no way compromises your individuality. In fact, it's actually the other way around. The more you conform to the world, the less you are truly you! The more you become a product of the world and pop culture, the more you become just like everybody else—assimilated into the masses. Yet the more you yield your life to God and become like His Son, the more He uses your unique character and personality traits to live out His purpose through you. It's an amazing but wonderful paradox.

So, as you study these pages, don't be threatened by a lifestyle that you think "isn't you!" Rather, I challenge you to take a submitted approach. Decide now that you will gladly and willingly live out what God desires, from a sincere and pure heart. Decide that you will embrace change. Decide that you will not only *do* what God wants, but that you will do it from a right heart! Nothing could be more pleasing to Him, and nothing could make you a more unique individual as a part of God's eternal purpose and plan!

God designed the Christian life to be a condition of the heart that shows up in a lifestyle. He commands us to keep right hearts with Him, and He commands us to do some things for Him. He desires that our *doing* flow from our *being*! And both are vital to Him!

In the coming pages, you will be challenged to "step it up"—to be some things and to do some things that are very different from the world and even from many who call themselves Christians.

Each chapter and each point is supported with Scripture—some of which modern Christendom has all but ignored. I challenge you to read and study with an open heart. Decide now that where God's Word contradicts your lifestyle—His Word will win. No argument. No fight. No rationalization or excuses. Just choose to let God be God.

A godly life is a good life. Why Christians have stopped believing that in recent years, I don't understand. But I believe it's time that we reclaim biblical values in our outward lifestyle. I believe that "have it your way" Christianity is empty, frustrating, self-centered, fruitless, and pointless. And those who have bought into it are soon to be disappointed. Even non-Christians know that the Christian life is a life that should be different! God teaches us in His Word that we are to be different—by His design. And living a life that is different by design is not as terrible as some would have you think! In fact, it's actually still the best way to live life. I pray this study will help you discover this to be true!

Don't be afraid to have a Christian life that involves "doing" which flows from "being." And don't be afraid to have a Christian life that is truly conformed to the image (the outward manifestation) of Christ. The Christian life truly is more than a mere condition of the heart. While it starts in the heart, it must then flow into every act, every word, every thought, every deed, every attitude. It flows into every little corner of life. It touches every part of our mannerisms, our behavior, and our lifestyle. It is not a compartmentalized, segmented life. The Christian life is about *all* of life. It is about living out every day and every moment on every level for the pleasure of Jesus Christ. It is about *doing* everything He said to do—from a right heart.

May these chapters help you rediscover that God created you to be "different by design" and may you truly discover that a godly life is still a good life!

Different by Design
A Life Becoming of the Faith of the Gospel

"Only let your conversation be as it becometh the gospel of Christ: that whether I come and see you, or else be absent, I may hear of your affairs, that ye stand fast in one spirit, with one mind striving together for the faith of the gospel;"—PHILIPPIANS 1:27

Exposing the Culture Creature

Hey, I hate to tell you this, but your culture has been lying to you! In an effort to rob you of some of the basic dignity and joy of life, Satan has trapped many people in a lifestyle that leads nowhere fast. For instance, I'm not against video games—but when is the last time a video game helped you become someone better? Video games don't grow you—they entertain you. They cause you to vegetate rather than mature. When not controlled, they become addicting. They hold you hostage and keep you from developing in some very important areas. The same could be said for many things that pop-culture crams down your throat—from music to videos to movies to a zillion other time wasters.

Along with that, culture has lied to you about "the good life"! Over the years, a lot of teenagers have said to me, "Hey, I'm just tired of being *good*." That statement doesn't make sense to me! Good is good! Bad is bad. Why would someone just want a "bad life"?

When I go to a restaurant, I don't say to the waiter, "Hey, bring me the worst thing on the menu!" When I celebrate a birthday, I don't hope to get cruddy gifts! When I have a family day with my kids, I don't say, "Hey guys, what's the worst thing we could do today?"

No, I'm on a quest for good—good food, good gifts, good friends, good fun, and good family time. So when did "good" become "bad"!? It doesn't make sense. In today's culture the sloppier you dress, the better. The more your hair is messed up, the cooler. The meaner you are to people, the better. The more crude and tasteless you can be, the funnier. The worse shape your life is in, the more acceptable you are to others. I guess misery just loves company!

The sad truth is this: the worse shape your life is in, the more miserable you are as a person. That's the bottom line. Bad is still bad. A *bad* life leads to *bad* things with *bad* consequences. To the contrary, a *good* life still leads to *good* things with *good* consequences. So, do you want a good life with good consequences or a bad life with bad consequences? It doesn't take a rocket scientist to figure this out!

So in the middle of a culture that is trying to dumb you down, keep you childish, and make your life worse and worse, I challenge you to be different—different by design. I challenge you to shake off the trappings of culture and choose God's way of life—choose the good life. You will discover that the good life is GOOD! Living for God is not drudgery, and living God's way, while it involves some decisions and some sacrifice, is well worth it!

What you are about to study is meant to help you choose to live differently. This study will cause you to seriously think about the way you live, the way you dress, the way you talk, and the relationships you maintain. Believe it or not, God is interested in all of these things, and He instructs us in each of these areas.

You will either live your life culture's way or God's way. You will either choose the "good life" or the "bad life." I challenge you to go with God. Reject culture and conform to Jesus Christ. Make Him your God. Decide to live the way He wants you to. I promise—He will make it worth it!

Let's start discovering that a godly life is a good life! And stop being tired of "being good." Good is GOOD!

Different by Design

Welcome to "Different by Design—Discovering That a Godly Life Is a Good Life." This book/study will take you on a journey of personal growth and development. The goal of this study is to help you to counteract the pull of culture towards a lifestyle that is less and less godly. The goal is to help you to develop a heart for God and an outward life that is "becoming" of the faith of the Gospel—that we would learn to "walk worthy" of our calling.

In this first chapter, we want to prepare our hearts to understand why our "lifestyle" is so important in the eyes of God and in the eyes of this world. After all, God sees the heart, right? If He sees our heart, why should we concern ourselves with the outward performance or appearance?

Let's discover some basic principles that will help us have a right perspective on what God desires to do in our lives through this study.

1. God Sees and Cares about the Condition of Our Hearts (Inward)

> *"Holding faith, and a good conscience; which some having put away concerning faith have made shipwreck:"*—1 TIMOTHY 1:19

> *"But the LORD said unto Samuel, Look not on his countenance, or on the height of his stature; because I have refused him: for the LORD seeth not as man seeth; for man looketh on the outward appearance, but the LORD looketh on the heart."*—1 SAMUEL 16:7

These verses teach us that God is first concerned with the condition of our hearts before Him. He sees every inward part, and He desires for our conscience—our inward man—to be right and growing.

2. God Sees and Cares about the Condition of Our Lifestyles (Outward)

> *"Let us walk honestly, as in the day; not in rioting and drunkenness, not in chambering and wantonness, not in strife and envying."*
> —ROMANS 13:13

> *"That ye would walk worthy of God, who hath called you unto his kingdom and glory."*
> —1 THESSALONIANS 2:12

"For this is the will of God, even your sanctification, that ye should abstain from fornication: That every one of you should know how to possess his vessel in sanctification and honour;"—1 THESSALONIANS 4:3–4

"For God hath not called us unto uncleanness, but unto holiness."—1 THESSALONIANS 4:7

Each of these verses refers to the fact that God also cares about our outward life—our "conversation" or our "walk." He makes it clear in Scripture that though He sees the heart, He is also intimately interested in the way we live our lives outwardly. Our walk or our conversation includes our dress, our attitudes, our appearance, our words, our friends, our behavior, and our communications.

3. God Wants Us to Care about Both Our Hearts and Our Lifestyles (Both)

"And every man that striveth for the mastery is temperate in all things. Now they do it to obtain a corruptible crown; but we an incorruptible."
—1 CORINTHIANS 9:25

"That ye might walk worthy of the Lord unto all pleasing, being fruitful in every good work, and increasing in the knowledge of God;"
—COLOSSIANS 1:10

"Let no man despise thy youth; but be thou an example of the believers, in word, in conversation, in charity, in spirit, in faith, in purity."—1 TIMOTHY 4:12

"Now the end of the commandment is charity out of a pure heart, and of a good conscience, and of faith unfeigned:"—1 TIMOTHY 1:5

"Seeing ye have purified your souls in obeying the truth through the Spirit unto unfeigned love of the brethren, see that ye love one another with a pure heart fervently:"—1 PETER 1:22

Temperate · adj. · showing moderation or self-restraint

The Bible uses the word *temperate*, which literally means "self restraint." God is teaching us that we should care enough about our hearts and our lives that we restrain ourselves in "all things." In other words, He calls us to make careful choices about our lives because we're living for a higher call.

The above verse from Colossians teaches us to grow in the knowledge of God—that's inward, as well as to be "fruitful in every good work"—that's outward!

The verse from 1 Timothy teaches us to be an example—to outwardly display a godly lifestyle that flows from a faith-filled, pure heart! Paul also teaches us in this book to have a visible faith that others can see, but to make sure it is "unfeigned"—not fake or put on as an outward show!

Finally, the verse from 1 Peter teaches us to purify our souls—that's inward, and then to love one another fervently—that's outward!

These verses and many others teach that God desires for you to have both a pure heart and a godly lifestyle at the same time!

4. God Is Not Pleased with Mere Outward Conformity to Christ

"Wherefore the Lord said, Forasmuch as this people draw near me with their mouth, and with their lips do honour me, but have removed their heart far from me, and their fear toward me is taught by the precept of men:"—ISAIAH 29:13

"He answered and said unto them, Well hath Esaias prophesied of you hypocrites, as it is written, This people honoureth me with their lips, but their heart is far from me."—MARK 7:6

"This people draweth nigh unto me with their mouth, and honoureth me with their lips; but their heart is far from me."—MATTHEW 15:8

God is not interested in mere "appearances" of godliness or purity! He isn't impressed by our mere conformity to a system! God even instructed His people in the Old Testament to stop their outward forms of worship because their hearts were cold and distant.

It is important that you approach this study with a right heart—that you not merely conform, but that you truly desire for God to change you from within. It is vital that you desire to be a mature Christian—understanding the inward and the outward life that Christ desires to produce in you.

5. God Desires Outward Change to Be Produced in the Heart First

"A new heart also will I give you, and a new spirit will I put within you: and I will take away the

7

stony heart out of your flesh, and I will give you an heart of flesh."—EZEKIEL 36:26

"Being confident of this very thing, that he which hath begun a good work in you will perform it until the day of Jesus Christ:"—PHILIPPIANS 1:6

God always begins His work on the inside! He never tells us to change the outside without first reflecting His change on the inside. It is God's desire that every outward change in your lifestyle would flow from His work of grace in your heart.

6. When God Changes My Heart, His Changes Will Be Outwardly Visible

"But the fruit of the Spirit is love, joy, peace, longsuffering, gentleness, goodness, faith,"
—GALATIANS 5:22

"(For the fruit of the Spirit is in all goodness and righteousness and truth;)"—EPHESIANS 5:9

"For I have given you an example, that ye should do as I have done to you."—JOHN 13:15

"Yea, a man may say, Thou hast faith, and I have works: shew me thy faith without thy works, and I will shew thee my faith by my works."
—JAMES 2:18

"A good man out of the good treasure of his heart bringeth forth that which is good; and an evil man out of the evil treasure of his heart bringeth forth that which is evil: for of the abundance of the heart his mouth speaketh."—LUKE 6:45

"Doth a fountain send forth at the same place sweet water and bitter? Can the fig tree, my brethren, bear olive berries? either a vine, figs? so can no fountain both yield salt water and fresh."—JAMES 3:11–12

It is impossible to be changed by God in your heart and not reflect that change in your life! The heart always reveals itself in the lifestyle. God's work within will always find its way to the surface.

Simply put—you can FAKE a right heart with God, but you can never HIDE a right heart with God! Everyone will know when you are right with God and living for Him from the heart!

In other words, you might be able to cover a defiled heart and fake godliness for a time, but a godly heart is never hidden by an ungodly lifestyle on the "outside."

7. God Offers His Power to Change My Inward and Outward Life

"For it is God which worketh in you both to will and to do of his good pleasure."—PHILIPPIANS 2:13

"Whereunto I also labour, striving according to his working, which worketh in me mightily."—COLOSSIANS 1:29

"And be not drunk with wine, wherein is excess; but be filled with the Spirit;"—EPHESIANS 5:18

"Now unto him that is able to do exceeding abundantly above all that we ask or think,

according to the power that worketh in us,"
—EPHESIANS 3:20

Each of these verses teaches us that God empowers change! He doesn't command us to change ourselves; He offers us His mighty power to bring about real change from within our hearts.

As we study these chapters, you must realize, it's not up to you to grow yourself! God stands ready to change you from within, if you will accept His invitation. Your responsibility is to yield to Him with an open heart—to have a heart attitude that could pray something like this:

"Lord, as I study and learn about a heart and life that is pleasing to my Saviour, I truly desire to be changed by your grace. Would you work in me through your power to live out the principles I will learn in these pages?"

Decide now that you will let God's power change you from within!

8. An Outward Christianity Driven by an Inward Sincerity Is Pleasing to God

"And beside this, giving all diligence, add to your faith virtue; and to virtue knowledge; And to knowledge temperance; and to temperance patience; and to patience godliness; And to godliness brotherly kindness; and to brotherly kindness charity. For if these things be in you, and abound, they make you that ye shall neither be barren nor unfruitful in the knowledge of our Lord Jesus Christ. But he that lacketh these things is blind, and cannot see afar off, and hath forgotten that he was purged from his old sins."—2 PETER 1:5–9

Masculinity
Qualities of a Godly Man

"Help, Lord; for the godly man ceaseth; for the faithful fail from among the children of men."—Psalm 12:1

"All scripture is given by inspiration of God, and is profitable for doctrine, for reproof, for correction, for instruction in righteousness: That the man of God may be perfect, throughly furnished unto all good works."—2 Timothy 3:16–17

True to Your Gender

Has it occurred to you lately that your culture is trying to make you dissatisfied with who God made you to be? As a man, culture would prefer that you have "alternative choices," that you be attracted to other men, that you pervert your God-given life role into something that will ultimately destroy you.

Whether perverting your passions or diverting your life direction, culture wants you to wish you were something or someone else.

The crazy thing is this—no matter what you do or decide, you will always be what God made you! God determined your gender, and He designed you on purpose for a purpose. Nothing you can do can change that. Even though culture tries, at the end of the day men are still men and women are still women.

One of the most blatant forms of rebellion against God is rebellion against your gender! Why? Because it resists God's basic and most foundational design. It says, "God, I refuse to be who you made me to be!" Satan wants you to shake your fist in God's face and resist the very design by which you were created. Tragically, this kind of rebellion produces the most desperate and miserable kind of life.

Good news—you were given your gender by God, and your specific design has a purpose in God's plan for your life and for eternity. You can silence the lies of culture and believe the voice of God. You can embrace the purpose for who God made you, and you can become a godly man!

If you haven't noticed lately, if you're a teenager, you're changing! The teen years are famous for that—change! During these years, your body grows, your attitude changes, your brain recreates itself, your voice changes, your schedule changes, your responsibilities increase, and on and on the list goes! From the time you turn twelve to the time you enter your twenties, life is like a non-stop roller-coaster ride of change. Sometimes that change can be stressful and even overwhelming.

One of the most important changes you are experiencing is that you are quickly becoming an adult. And you are deciding right now what kind of adult you will become. Today's challenge is first to embrace your gender! Recognize that you are a man by God's design. Second, the challenge is to understand God's purpose for your gender. God has created you specifically for a purpose, and His Word shows us that purpose.

Do you want a good adult life? Do you desire God's best? If so, then ask Him to help you become the godly man that He intends, and seek to understand what being a godly man really means.

Life is the happiest when you are being who God created you to be! Don't wish you were something or someone else. Don't buy into culture's lies. Decide that you will go with God and embrace your purpose in His plan.

Let's take a look at what God says about men and godliness!

What It Means to Be a Man

There is a great shortage in modern society of true character traits of godly manhood. Sure, there are plenty of men around, but few have been trained or taught what a true man really is. Godly manhood—or manhood the way God created and designed it to be, should be the heart's desire of every Christian man.

In the coming pages, we will study ten basic biblical principles that define a godly man. These principles are, in most ways, unique to "men," and we must ask God to form these qualities into our character and etch them onto our hearts.

As we study these principles, we must realize that these are foundational to who God made us to be—as men. We will never be more joyful, content, and fulfilled in our lives than when we are becoming the godly men that He intends for us to be.

What does it mean to be a man?

Many define manhood as gruffness, athleticism, roughness, crudeness, harshness, hardness, coldness, etc. In addition to this, many men today are dead, dry, passive, emotionless, passionless, silent, dull, and bored.

By God's grace, may we become men that are vibrant, full of life, full of responsiveness to God and to others. Let's discover ten biblical qualities of a godly man.

1. A Godly Person Accepts God's Different Design of Men and Women

"So God created man in his own image, in the image of God created he him; male and female created he them."—GENESIS 1:27

"Male and female created he them; and blessed them, and called their name Adam, in the day when they were created."—GENESIS 5:2

First, we must understand the basics of God's creation of men and women. Consider these points:

- ◆ God created men and women and made them distinctly different on purpose.
- ◆ God gave men and women very different capacities and roles in life.
- ◆ Culture has tried to destroy God's distinction between men and women.
- ◆ Culture distorts and perverts God's creation out of rebellion against Him.
- ◆ Satan wants to confuse you and does not want you to become a godly man.

If you listen to culture, you will not achieve the qualities we will study. If you allow God to grow you, these character traits will become foundational to your identity as a Christian man.

Don't buy the lie of the world. Differences between men and women are not about who is *better*, but rather about God's unique plan for each gender. Both genders are highly valuable in God's purpose for creation.

Be glad and thankful that God made you a man!

See yourself now, growing and becoming a godly man. Choose to become the man that God created you to become.

2. A Godly Man Understands That He Is Created for a Purpose

"Before I formed thee in the belly I knew thee; and before thou camest forth out of the womb I sanctified thee, and I ordained thee a prophet unto the nations."—JEREMIAH 1:5

"And I sought for a man among them, that should make up the hedge, and stand in the gap before me for the land, that I should not destroy it: but I found none."—EZEKIEL 22:30

"The steps of a good man are ordered by the LORD: and he delighteth in his way."—PSALM 37:23

"And when he had removed him, he raised up unto them David to be their king; to whom also he gave testimony, and said, I have found David the son of Jesse, a man after mine own heart, which shall fulfil all my will."—ACTS 13:22

God doesn't merely create men without a reason. He designed you, created you, and gave you a life calling—a purpose for living. You are here on earth on assignment from Him. He gives you the free will to accept or reject that assignment.

God's call upon your life must be chosen by faith, pursued with passion, discovered one step at a time, and lived out joyfully. His call upon your life perfectly matches your identity—who He made you to be, and only by living His purpose will you truly discover what abundant life is really all about.

A godly man recognizes that he belongs to God and that he was placed on this earth for a reason. He allows God to "order the steps" of his life. He lives to do God's will.

3. A Godly Man Knows How to Give Himself to Hard Work

"He also that is slothful in his work is brother to him that is a great waster."—PROVERBS 18:9

"Prepare thy work without, and make it fit for thyself in the field; and afterwards build thine house."—PROVERBS 24:27

"I went by the field of the slothful, and by the vineyard of the man void of understanding; And, lo, it was all grown over with thorns, and nettles had covered the face thereof, and the stone wall thereof was broken down. Then I saw, and considered it well: I looked upon it, and received instruction. Yet a little sleep, a little slumber, a little folding of the hands to sleep: So shall thy poverty come as one that

travelleth; and thy want as an armed man."
—PROVERBS 24:30–34

This principle began when God gave Adam the responsibility to keep and dress the garden and to name the animals. Every man is created to accomplish work. Every man will be given a work to do on this earth, and he should do it for the glory of God.

For young men, this work comes in the form of learning, growing, building, and developing knowledge and skill. This means accepting the challenges that lie before you—to do well in school, work hard on projects, give your best in sports and other opportunities. This means that whatever God has given you to do while you are young, you choose to do it with all your might. Over time, these responsibilities will become bigger and weightier!

Learning to work hard will serve you well all your life, as you are diligent in whatever work God gives you to do. Accept responsibility now, do your best, learn to work hard, and learn to enjoy working.

Godly men find great fulfillment in doing a job well and accomplishing something to the glory of God. Every work you do has the signature of your character upon it—whether it's mowing a lawn, writing a report, or cleaning the garage. Work hard and do your best. Leave a good reflection of your character in the completion of every sort of work you perform.

4. A Godly Man Learns How to Lead and Exert a Good Influence

"A good man out of the good treasure of the heart bringeth forth good things: and an evil

man out of the evil treasure bringeth forth evil things."—MATTHEW 12:35

"A good man sheweth favour, and lendeth: he will guide his affairs with discretion."
—PSALM 112:5

"Let love be without dissimulation. Abhor that which is evil; cleave to that which is good."
—ROMANS 12:9

Some young men have convinced themselves that they can merely exist without being an influence. Rather than shoulder the responsibilities of being a "good influence," they simply try to be neutral. This is impossible. Because you exist, you will be an influence. You will lead someone. You will either be a good or bad influence—you cannot be neutral. If you fail to intentionally be a good influence, you will, by default, be a bad one.

Godly men don't try to avoid having influence. You cannot avoid being an influence on others. You can only choose to steward your influence—to use it. Godly men decide to use whatever influence they have for as much good as possible.

We will talk about leadership and influence in another chapter, but recognize now that godly men don't fear leading, and they don't run from good! They embrace good, and lead others to do the same!

5. A Godly Man Accepts His Responsibility to Provide for Others

"But if any provide not for his own, and specially for those of his own house, he hath

denied the faith, and is worse than an infidel."
—1 TIMOTHY 5:8

"A good man leaveth an inheritance to his children's children: and the wealth of the sinner is laid up for the just."—PROVERBS 13:22

God has given men the responsibility to provide for their families. Though you may still be a young man, it is vital that you understand this principle and embrace it. You will soon shoulder the responsibility of caring and providing for others.

For most men, this is a constant pressure and burden, but godly men rest upon the Lord and trust Him to guide and to provide. Ultimately, the Lord will always bless and provide for the man who is trusting Him.

Your call to provide for those you love should cause you to fall in love with God and follow Him passionately now! He will never fail you. Don't fear this responsibility; look forward to it.

If and when God blesses you with a family, do your absolute best to take care of them! This is your God-given responsibility. Even if your wife works or has an income, the responsibility to provide for the family will rest squarely on your shoulders.

6. A Godly Man Accepts His Responsibility to Protect Others

"Be sober, be vigilant; because your adversary the devil, as a roaring lion, walketh about, seeking whom he may devour:"—1 PETER 5:8

> "Likewise, ye husbands, dwell with them according to knowledge, giving honour unto the wife, as unto the weaker vessel, and as being heirs together of the grace of life; that your prayers be not hindered."—1 PETER 3:7

The Bible teaches that our wives are "weaker vessels." The Bible also teaches that we are to be sober and vigilant against our enemy—Satan.

As a man, you will be the spiritual leader and protector of your home one day. This is God's design. You are the spiritual wall of protection for your wife and children! If you are godly and right with the Lord, Satan will not be able to get past your prayers in attacking your family.

Now is the time to become a godly spiritual warrior who will fight spiritually for your wife and children! Grow strong in God's grace, and prepare for this vital role of Christian manhood.

7. A Godly Man Knows How to Love and Serve God and Others

> "Husbands, love your wives, even as Christ also loved the church, and gave himself for it;" —EPHESIANS 5:25

> "And, ye fathers, provoke not your children to wrath: but bring them up in the nurture and admonition of the Lord."—EPHESIANS 6:4

> "Fathers, provoke not your children to anger, lest they be discouraged."—COLOSSIANS 3:21

> "Husbands, love your wives, and be not bitter against them."—COLOSSIANS 3:19

Men are made to love. Our hearts are designed to love, and God commands us to love Him and others. Our love should compel us to serve God and others.

Often, men love the wrong things—games, sports, fun, pleasure. When we love the wrong things, we become wimps—unfulfilled and not respected. But when we love the right things, we become strong, courageous and viewed as men of integrity.

God commands us to first love Him, then our wives and children, then each other! You will know that you are becoming a man of God when you begin to love the way that Jesus would. Love is sacrificial, serving, giving—it is laying down your life for someone else. Love lives for another and lives to serve another.

If you will be a godly man, you will have to choose to love the things that God loves.

8. A Godly Man Understands Commitment to God and Family

"And if it seem evil unto you to serve the Lord, *choose you this day whom ye will serve; whether the gods which your fathers served that were on the other side of the flood, or the gods of the Amorites, in whose land ye dwell: but as for me and my house, we will serve the* Lord.*"*—Joshua 24:15

"My heart is fixed, O God, my heart is fixed: I will sing and give praise."—Psalm 57:7

"Most men will proclaim every one his own goodness: but a faithful man who can find?"
—Proverbs 20:6

"Except the LORD build the house, they labour in vain that build it: except the LORD keep the city, the watchman waketh but in vain."
—PSALM 127:1

"For this cause shall a man leave his father and mother, and shall be joined unto his wife, and they two shall be one flesh."—EPHESIANS 5:31

God has called men to commitment! Yet, commitment is completely against what our world teaches us! The world teaches us to "try and see if it will work out for me." The world teaches us to avoid commitment.

If you want to be a godly man, you will have to learn commitment. Commit yourself completely to God FIRST! By learning now how to be committed to God, you will learn how to keep every other future commitment of your life! Commitment to God first is the training ground for a committed marriage, family, and future.

Commitment means that you will never give yourself the option of quitting on God or on a godly commitment.

9. A Godly Man Finds His Strength and Stability in the Lord

"I will say of the LORD, He is my refuge and my fortress: my God; in him will I trust."
—PSALM 91:2

"Through wisdom is an house builded; and by understanding it is established:"
—PROVERBS 24:3

"But they that wait upon the LORD shall renew their strength; they shall mount up with wings

*as eagles; they shall run, and not be weary; and
they shall walk, and not faint."*—Isaiah 40:31

*"O Lord, my strength, and my fortress,
and my refuge in the day of affliction..."*
—Jeremiah 16:19

*"Thou therefore, my son, be strong in the grace
that is in Christ Jesus."*—2 Timothy 2:1

*"Be not carried about with divers and strange
doctrines. For it is a good thing that the heart
be established with grace; not with meats, which
have not profited them that have been occupied
therein."*—Hebrews 13:9

*"That Christ may dwell in your hearts by faith;
that ye, being rooted and grounded in love,"*
—Ephesians 3:17

*"Rooted and built up in him, and stablished in
the faith, as ye have been taught, abounding
therein with thanksgiving."*—Colossians 2:7

The life of a godly man will include pressure, tension,
stress, burdens, and trials. Yet a godly man will bear these
things not only for himself, but for his family and others. God
has not called us into these things alone. God offers us His
strength, His stability. God offers to root us, ground us, and
establish us in Him!

Godly men embrace pressure and burdens as a part of
God's call upon their lives. They find strength in their private
personal walk with God, and they renew their strength in God.
Godly men are not afraid of some pressure or stress. They step
into the battle, not *away*. They get *onto* the playing field, not

off. They courageously face scary situations rather than freeze in fear. They press on against opposition rather than cave in.

As you become a man of God, you must find your strength and courage in Christ. He will infuse your heart with the kind of manhood that will face life head on, leading and loving those you influence.

This courage and stability will become an anchor for your family, friends, and others! People are looking for this kind of manhood!

10. A Godly Man Will Be Greatly Blessed and Favored by God

"A good man obtaineth favour of the Lord: *but a man of wicked devices will he condemn."*
—Proverbs 12:2

"For thou, Lord, *wilt bless the righteous; with favour wilt thou compass him as with a shield."*—Psalm 5:12

"So shalt thou find favour and good understanding in the sight of God and man."
—Proverbs 3:4

"He that diligently seeketh good procureth favour: but he that seeketh mischief, it shall come unto him."—Proverbs 11:27

"And Jesus increased in wisdom and stature, and in favour with God and man."
—Luke 2:52

The Bible is clear that God plays favorites! God blesses the man who chooses godliness! He favors those who walk rightly for His glory!

The favor of God is more valuable than any other thing in life! If you choose godly manhood, you are choosing God's favor and blessing! How this will show up in your future is up to God, but you can be sure that God will be good to His Word—He blesses those that honor Him!

Conclusion

> *"That thou mayest walk in the way of good men, and keep the paths of the righteous."*
> —PROVERBS 2:20

As men, we were designed to have these qualities! When we live out these qualities, we feel strengthened, affirmed, worthwhile, and fulfilled in our God-given purpose in life. When we do not live out these qualities, we feel frustrated, lost, purposeless, and worthless.

Plan to make life a series of great memories! Let your life be a journey into these qualities by the grace of God!

Look forward to a rewarded, blessed life as you seek to honor the Lord!

Questions for Personal Study
Masculinity

1. Read the ten character traits and pray now that God will help you become a godly man by His grace.

2. List some ways that you see culture trying to erase the differences between men and women.

3. Describe and write out what the world thinks is manly that doesn't match up with God's definition.

4. List a few godly character traits of manhood that you feel you should focus on developing in your life.

5. Write out and memorize Proverbs 12:2 regarding God's favor upon good men.

Femininity
Qualities of a Godly Woman

"Who can find a virtuous woman? for her price is far above rubies."—PROVERBS 31:10

True to Your Gender

(If you already read the "True to Your Gender" portion of the last chapter, you should skip ahead to the next section.)

Has it occurred to you lately that your culture is trying to make you dissatisfied with who God made you to be? As a woman, culture would have you to think that unless you establish a career making as much money as men, you are somehow a failure and lacking in life.

Whether perverting your passions or diverting your life direction, culture wants you to wish you were something or someone else.

The crazy thing is this—no matter what you do or decide, you will always be what God made you! God determined your gender, and He designed you on purpose for a purpose.

Nothing you can do can change that. Even though culture tries, at the end of the day men are still men, and women are still women.

One of the most blatant forms of rebellion against God is rebellion against your gender! Why? Because it resists God's basic and most foundational design. It says, "God, I refuse to be who you made me to be!" Satan wants you to shake your fist in God's face and resist the very design by which you were created. Tragically, this kind of rebellion produces the most desperate and miserable kind of life.

Good news—you were given your gender by God, and your specific design has a purpose in God's plan for your life and for eternity. You can silence the lies of culture and believe the voice of God. You can embrace the purpose for whom God made you, and you can become a godly woman!

If you haven't noticed lately, if you're a teenager, you're changing! The teen years are famous for that—change! During these years, your body grows, your attitude changes, your brain recreates itself, your schedule changes, your responsibilities increase, and on and on the list goes! From the time you turn twelve to the time you enter your twenties, life is like a non-stop roller-coaster ride of change. Sometimes that change can be stressful and even overwhelming.

One of the most important changes is that you are quickly becoming an adult. And you are deciding right now what kind of adult you will become. Today's challenge is first to embrace your gender! Recognize that you are a woman by God's design. Second, the challenge is to understand God's purpose for your gender. God has created you specifically for a purpose, and His Word shows us that purpose.

Do you want a good adult life? Do you desire God's best? If so, then ask Him to help you become the godly woman that He intends, and seek to understand what being a godly woman really means.

Life is the happiest when you are being who God created you to be! Don't wish you were something or someone else. Don't buy into culture's lies. Decide that you will go with God and embrace your purpose in His plan.

Let's take a look at what God says about women and godliness!

What It Means to Be a Godly Woman

There is a great shortage in modern society of godly women. Sure, there are plenty of women around, but few have been trained or taught what a true woman really is. Godly womanhood—or womanhood the way God created and designed it to be, should be the heart's desire of every Christian lady.

In this chapter, we will study ten basic biblical principles that define a godly woman. These principles are, in most ways, unique to "women," and each lady must ask God to form these qualities into her character and etch them onto her heart.

As these principles are studied, each lady must realize that these principles are foundational to who God made her to be. A lady will never be more joyful, content, and fulfilled in her life than when she is becoming the godly lady that God intends for her to be.

What does it mean to be a lady?

Many define womanhood as a certain age, appearance, level of responsibility, independence, etc. In addition to this, many women today are unfulfilled, empty, purposeless, and aimless. They survive life rather than savor and enjoy it!

By God's grace, may you become a lady that is vibrant, full of life, full of responsiveness to God and to others. Let's discover ten biblical qualities of a godly woman.

1. A Godly Person Accepts God's Different Design of Men and Women

> "*So God created man in his own image, in the image of God created he him; male and female created he them.*"—GENESIS 1:27

> "*Male and female created he them; and blessed them, and called their name Adam, in the day when they were created.*"—GENESIS 5:2

First, we must understand the basics of God's creation of men and women. Consider these points:

+ God created men and women and made them distinctly different on purpose.
+ God gave men and women very different capacities and roles in life.
+ Culture has tried to destroy God's distinction between men and women.
+ Culture distorts and perverts God's creation out of rebellion against Him.
+ Satan wants to confuse you and does not want you to become a godly woman.

If you listen to culture, you will not achieve the qualities that we will study. If you allow God to grow you, these character traits will become foundational to your identity as a Christian woman.

Don't buy the lie of the world. Differences between men and women are not about who is *better*, but rather about God's unique plan for each gender. Both genders are highly valuable in God's purpose for creation.

Be glad and thankful that God made you a woman!

See yourself as a woman—growing and becoming a godly lady. Choose that you will become the woman that God created you to become!

2. A Godly Woman Is a Supporter and Encourager to Others

> *"The heart of her husband doth safely trust in her, so that he shall have no need of spoil. She will do him good and not evil all the days of her life."*—PROVERBS 31:11–12

> *"She openeth her mouth with wisdom; and in her tongue is the law of kindness."*—PROVERBS 31:26

> *"But refuse profane and old wives' fables, and exercise thyself rather unto godliness."*—1 TIMOTHY 4:7

> *"And withal they learn to be idle, wandering about from house to house; and not only idle, but tattlers also and busybodies, speaking things which they ought not. I will therefore that the younger women marry, bear children, guide the house, give none occasion to the adversary to speak reproachfully."*—1 TIMOTHY 5:13–14

> *"To be discreet, chaste, keepers at home, good, obedient to their own husbands, that the word of God be not blasphemed."*—TITUS 2:5

From the beginning of time, God created women to support and encourage. He has gifted you, as a woman, with the ability to build up, strengthen, support, and encourage others. The world tells you to live for yourself, but God calls you to a wonderful, rewarding role of support, care, encouragement and love!

This is not a lesser role; it is the high calling and design of almighty God! As His unique and wonderful creation, He has enabled you to fulfill the specific purpose of supporting and encouraging others!

Embrace this character trait and decide to use your heart and spirit for the purpose that God created you!

3. A Godly Woman Has a Meek and a Quiet Spirit in Heart and Character

"But let it be the hidden man of the heart, in that which is not corruptible, even the ornament of a meek and quiet spirit, which is in the sight of God of great price."—1 PETER 3:4

"The aged women likewise, that they be in behaviour as becometh holiness, not false accusers, not given to much wine, teachers of good things;"—TITUS 2:3

Godly ladies find delight in being pure in heart, meek in spirit, and quiet in their person. This doesn't mean that a woman's input isn't valuable or that a woman cannot speak up, laugh, or enjoy life. It simply means that a godly woman isn't known for being loud, boisterous, overbearing, and forward! A godly woman isn't seeking to be the center of attention or seeking to dominate a conversation or social circumstance.

Godly women find contentment in Christ, attention from the love of God, and a heart fulfillment in their walk with the Lord that allows them to be "meek and quiet." They are known for their sweet, humble disposition and their godly, holy lifestyle. This doesn't mean you squelch or change your true personality, but rather you use your God-given personality to honor the Lord—you submit your personality to His control.

What are you known for? Do people know you for your flirtatiousness? Your loudness? Your desire to be the center of attention? Your overbearing personality? Each of these personality traits becomes a tremendous weakness when it is not controlled by the Holy Spirit.

4. A Godly Woman Allows Her Outward Beauty to Reflect Her True Heart

"While they behold your chaste conversation coupled with fear. Whose adorning let it not be that outward adorning of plaiting the hair, and of wearing of gold, or of putting on of apparel; But let it be the hidden man of the heart, in that which is not corruptible, even the ornament of a meek and quiet spirit, which is in the sight of God of great price."—1 PETER 3:2–4

The world would have you completely focus on your exterior appearance—your weight, your figure, your hair, your makeup, your clothing. There's nothing wrong with looking nice, but the focus of a godly woman begins with the heart! Surface beauty that isn't backed up by a godly heart ultimately becomes something that you will resent and for which you will be resented. Like a thin layer of paint on an old piece of rotten wood—the inside will eventually come out and be known.

God calls you to develop your heart for Him first! Just as Moses' countenance revealed that he had been in the presence of God, even so, a godly woman's heart will always show in her appearance! A pure heart will be revealed in a beauty that makeup and jewelry cannot produce!

Godliness in the heart produces a joyful countenance that is more beautiful than anything the world can produce.

Simply put, you will either try to decorate yourself to achieve artificial, temporary beauty—to make yourself feel temporarily good about yourself; or you will develop a pure heart and a right heart with God, and as a byproduct, your countenance will have a spiritual beauty that cannot be replaced!

5. A Godly Woman Gives Her Life to Serve and Care for Others

"She seeketh wool, and flax, and worketh willingly with her hands. She is like the merchants' ships; she bringeth her food from afar. She riseth also while it is yet night, and giveth meat to her household, and a portion to her maidens. She considereth a field, and buyeth it: with the fruit of her hands she planteth a vineyard. She girdeth her loins with strength, and strengtheneth her arms. She perceiveth that her merchandise is good: her candle goeth not out by night. She layeth her hands to the spindle, and her hands hold the distaff. She stretcheth out her hand to the poor; yea, she reacheth forth her hands to the needy. She is not afraid of the snow for her household: for all her household are clothed

with scarlet. She maketh herself coverings of tapestry; her clothing is silk and purple. Her husband is known in the gates, when he sitteth among the elders of the land. She maketh fine linen, and selleth it; and delivereth girdles unto the merchant."—PROVERBS 31:13–24

"*Greet Mary, who bestowed much labour on us.*"—ROMANS 16:6

"*That they may teach the young women to be sober, to love their husbands, to love their children,*"—TITUS 2:4

As a woman, you have been gifted with the ability to care and serve. This is a God-given nature that comes from deep in the heart! It is a precious gift from God. It can be used to bless, comfort, and care for those you love for the rest of your life, but you must first embrace this gift and choose to develop it for God's glory.

The world would tempt you to toss this gift aside so that you can live for self. Many women sacrifice this life-calling so they can pursue a lesser career or self-interest. The highest calling you can fulfill is the calling of God. Be thankful that God has given you the privilege of caring for others. Develop your abilities to care. Learn to serve. Volunteer to serve. Do everything you can to honor the Lord by loving, serving, and caring for others.

6. A Godly Woman Finds Her Strength and Emotional Dependence upon the Lord

"*Strength and honour are her clothing; and she shall rejoice in time to come.*"—PROVERBS 31:25

"Favour is deceitful, and beauty is vain: but a woman that feareth the LORD, she shall be praised."—PROVERBS 31:30

A godly woman has an inner strength and stability that only comes from the Lord. The world would tempt you to seek acceptance from friends, guys, and other places. While these things promise to make you feel fulfilled in your heart, they only leave you empty and longing for God. All the while, you have a loving Heavenly Father who promises to give you His strength. He will settle your heart, fill your soul, and strengthen your life. He is everything your heart truly craves.

Where do you find your stability and strength right now? From friends? From a man? From your appearance? The Bible says that these things are deceitful and vain. God will not "play with your heart" the way the world will! He loves you and will only strengthen you and settle you.

Godly women have an inner strength that can only come from private time with God. Seek Him, and let Him prepare you for a life of love and joy that flow first from Him!

7. A Godly Woman Honors the Lord in Her Heart and Lifestyle

"And Mary said, Behold the handmaid of the Lord; be it unto me according to thy word. And the angel departed from her."—LUKE 1:38

"And Mary said, My soul doth magnify the Lord, And my spirit hath rejoiced in God my Saviour." —LUKE 1:46–47

"In like manner also, that women adorn themselves in modest apparel, with shamefacedness and

sobriety; not with broided hair, or gold, or pearls, or costly array;"—1 TIMOTHY 2:9

"Even so must their wives be grave, not slanderers, sober, faithful in all things."—1 TIMOTHY 3:11

Mary's words to God reflect the heart of a godly woman: "Behold the handmaid of the Lord; be it unto me according to thy word." Mary saw that she was God's, first! She chose to honor the Lord even when her life was not turning out the way she expected!

Grave · adj. · to be honorable and honest

Paul wrote to Timothy that both the inner life and the outward appearance should honor the Lord. The word *grave* in 1 Timothy 3:11 literally means "to be honorable and honest."

There are so many ways in which women today are dishonoring themselves and the Lord! We will study many of these in the coming pages, but this is the foundational attitude of the heart—a godly woman desires to honor the Lord both inwardly and outwardly.

Do you view your life as your own? Are you demanding, overbearing, self-centered? A godly woman recognizes that she is "the handmaid of the Lord"—a servant of God first and foremost.

How would your life be different tomorrow if you really chose to honor the Lord in everything to the best of your ability?

8. A Godly Woman Prepares Her Life for Her Lord, her Husband, and Her Children

"That they may teach the young women to be sober, to love their husbands, to love their children,"—TITUS 2:4

"Likewise, ye wives, be in subjection to your own husbands; that, if any obey not the word, they also may without the word be won by the conversation of the wives;"—1 PETER 3:1

"For after this manner in the old time the holy women also, who trusted in God, adorned themselves, being in subjection unto their own husbands:"—1 PETER 3:5

"Wives, submit yourselves unto your own husbands, as it is fit in the Lord."—COLOSSIANS 3:18

"Wives, submit yourselves unto your own husbands, as unto the Lord."—EPHESIANS 5:22

If you are a young woman, this might seem a little bit premature, but nothing could be further from the truth. God is preparing you right now for a life of service to Him, most likely by fulfilling a future role as a wife and mother. Whatever roles God has planned for you, you can be sure He has a distinctly valuable purpose for your life for which He is preparing you now!

The words *submit* and *subjection* reflect a heart that willingly gives in for the good of others—a life lived for others in sincerity. This doesn't mean you will spend your life being a slave! It means exactly the opposite. As you give your life in service and sweet-spirited submission to God's authority in your life, you will be greatly blessed, favored, and honored by God!

The world doesn't want you to learn this truth! God calls you, now, to prepare for your family. How? By learning how to submit to God, serve Him, and love from the heart. The Bible commands younger women to learn these things early. No matter your age, give yourself to this preparation—bless your future family and ministry with a godly lady!

9. A Godly Woman Makes Her Home Her First Priority and a Special Place

"She looketh well to the ways of her household, and eateth not the bread of idleness."
—Proverbs 31:27

"To be discreet, chaste, keepers at home, good, obedient to their own husbands, that the word of God be not blasphemed."—Titus 2:5

No place in your future will present you with a greater opportunity to use your gifts of support and care than in your own home! As you prepare for your future, recognize that God's calling upon your life will most likely involve keeping a house, raising a family, supporting a husband, and making a wonderful home!

Decide now that you will not view this calling as any less important than a career! Decide that you will embrace God's role and God's design. Decide that your first priority, next to God, will be your home—your husband, your children, and your family environment.

10. A Godly Woman Will Be Honored and Cherished

"Her children arise up, and call her blessed; her husband also, and he praiseth her."
—PROVERBS 31:28

"Give her of the fruit of her hands; and let her own works praise her in the gates."—PROVERBS 31:31

There is great reward in being a godly woman! The world would try to convince you that loving your husband (or future husband), raising a family, caring for others, and serving Christ is somehow a less than respectable life. This just isn't true.

First of all, being a godly woman involves just as much hard work and labor as working outside the home would or as the roles of a godly man would. It's not that one is any better than the other; it's that they are different by design. You will never be more joyful than when you are living God's plan for you!

The reward comes as God favors those who obey Him. Your family will greatly honor you and bless you for your investment and sacrifice. The fruit of your life lived for God's glory will be an awesome reward!

Conclusion

"Who can find a virtuous woman? for her price is far above rubies."—PROVERBS 31:10

In today's culture, godly women are a rare treasure! And the devil is doing everything he can to keep you from becoming one. Think about these ten characteristics, and ask the Lord to mold you into the godly woman that He created you to be!

Look forward to a rewarded, blessed life as you seek to honor the Lord!

Questions for Personal Study
Femininity

1. Read the ten character traits and pray now that God will help you become a godly woman by His grace.

2. List some ways that you see culture trying to erase the differences between men and women.

3. Describe and write out what the world thinks a successful woman is and how it conflicts with God's definition.

4. List a few godly character traits that you feel you should focus on developing in your life.

5. Write out and memorize Proverbs 31:10 regarding the value of a virtuous woman.

CHAPTER FOUR

Modesty and Appropriateness

Dressing Appropriately as a Godly Person

"The life is more than meat, and the body is more than raiment."
—LUKE 12:23

"In like manner also, that women adorn themselves in modest apparel, with shamefacedness and sobriety; not with broided hair, or gold, or pearls, or costly array; But (which becometh women professing godliness) with good works."—1 TIMOTHY 2:9–10

In this lesson **M** refers to text that applies primarily to men. In this lesson **W** refers to text that applies primarily to women.

God Cares about What We Wear

Does God care about what you wear? I mean, really—isn't He too busy running the universe? Does how you dress really matter to Him? It does. He tells us this in His Word.

Once again, you will either be the victim of your culture or the champion of what is right in this matter. Hmmm—victim or champion?

What is culture teaching this generation about dress? Well let's think about it for a moment. Culture seems to say the following:

+ It has to be a popular name brand.
+ It should advertise some pop-culture brand, team, or icon.
+ If it's on a girl, it should be tight, low-cut, or revealing.
+ If it's on a guy, it should be baggy and sloppy looking.
+ If it's denim, it should be rough, worn, and with holes.
+ If it's dressy, it should be skimpy or see-through.
+ If it's tucked in, it's "out."
+ If it's for a man, it could look feminine.
+ If it's for a woman, it should get attention.
+ The sloppier looking, the cooler it is.
+ The tighter it is, the sexier—everybody needs to be sexy.

In short, if it's immodest, sloppy, trendy, faddish, or rebellious looking—it's in! And if you wear these things—you're in! What's that about? Come on! Please tell me you're slightly smarter than your culture thinks!

Okay—do you really want to be an automaton—mindlessly moved about by the dictator of pop-culture? Do you want pop-culture to drag you around with a ring in your nose telling you how to live and what to wear? Do you really want your dress choices in life to be determined by media fads and pop-stars who can't even stay out of rehab long enough to finish a concert tour? Is this really the crowd you want to model your life and future choices after? Obviously not.

So, once again, you have the world's system and God's teaching. Behind the world's system is a bunch of lies, deceptions, and a lifestyle that will lead you seriously downhill. Behind God's teaching you have a loving Heavenly Father who longs to bless your life and future and who longs to fulfill your heart's biggest desires.

Yes, God cares about our dress choices, and He gives us a Bible full of guiding principles upon which to base these choices. This is big stuff, and this chapter will challenge you to really think. What you wear is much more than a matter of rules or simple decisions. This isn't about just "doing what you're told."

No, we're going to dig a lot deeper than that. We're going to actually discover the serious heart of God on this matter. We're going to uncover the principles that form our beliefs and then our choices. It's one thing to say, "Dress modestly!" It's another thing entirely to consider the wealth of information God gives us behind that one statement. There are some really great reasons why you should choose to dress God's way, and we're about to find out what they are!

Stop finding your identity in what you wear. That's what everybody else does. You are more than what you wear. In fact, what you wear is actually a reflection of who you really are. We'll see more about that in a moment. Find your security—your identity—in your relationship with God, not in the labels hanging in your closet!

The great news is, you don't have to be super-geek in your dress just because you're a Christian. It's not like God is asking you to wear a white robe (at least not yet) all the time! Should you dress different than the world dictates? Yes. Should your principles be determined by God and not by your favorite clothing store at the mall? Yes. Do you have to be a total, out-of-style loser? No.

The simple fact is, dress is important. What you wear matters to God, and if you love Him, then you should ask Him, "God what do You want me to wear? How do You want me to dress? What do my dress choices really mean? What does my clothing reveal about who I really am?"

These are huge questions with Bible answers just ahead— let's get started!

What God Says about Clothing

We established in study one that God cares intimately about both your heart and your outward conversation or "lifestyle." He cares about how you appear to others—how you live, what you wear, what you say, how you behave, etc. In this chapter, we will study God's particular instructions and principles regarding how you dress as His child.

The general attitude of most people is that we belong to ourselves—it's our body; we can do or wear what we want! But this is not the teaching of God's Word for His children. In these pages, you will discover many Bible references to clothing that you perhaps never considered.

It might just surprise you what God really has to say about what you wear! Are you ready to hear from God and to obey Him? I hope so.

1.   The Way You Dress Always Matters to God

> *"I will greatly rejoice in the LORD, my soul shall be*
> *joyful in my God; for he hath clothed me with the*
> *garments of salvation, he hath covered me with the*

robe of righteousness, as a bridegroom decketh himself with ornaments, and as a bride adorneth herself with her jewels."—ISAIAH 61:10

"Wherefore, if God so clothe the grass of the field, which to day is, and to morrow is cast into the oven, shall he not much more clothe you, O ye of little faith?"—MATTHEW 6:30

Matthew 6:30 teaches us that it is God who desires to "clothe us." In other words, God desires to provide the clothing I wear just as He provides everything else in my life.

Though Isaiah is referencing salvation as a "clothing" or "garment" or "robe of righteousness"—this verse clearly references my salvation in a word picture of something worn outwardly. A garment is something that clothes the outward body, not the inward life.

We already know that God desires for our lifestyles to reflect our salvation, but the clothing we wear is a huge part of that lifestyle. What we wear should reflect the fact that Christ lives in us.

Simply put, I should be willing to identify my life as a Christian through my appearance. What I wear matters to God because it either reflects Him or it doesn't. Are you willing to honor God by choosing clothing that pleases Him?

2. The Way You Dress Identifies Your Character and Level of Respect

W *"While they behold your chaste conversation coupled with fear. Whose adorning let it not be that outward adorning of plaiting the hair, and of wearing of gold, or of putting on of apparel;"*—1 PETER 3:2–3

> *"And as they departed, Jesus began to say unto the multitudes concerning John, What went ye out into the wilderness to see? A reed shaken with the wind? But what went ye out for to see? A man clothed in soft raiment? behold, they that wear soft clothing are in kings' houses. But what went ye out for to see? A prophet? yea, I say unto you, and more than a prophet."*
> —MATTHEW 11:7–9

> *"And, behold, there met him a woman with the attire of an harlot, and subtil of heart."*
> —PROVERBS 7:10

These verses are very clear.

In 1 Peter, ladies are commanded to focus more on the heart and less on the outward "adorning." In other words, your heart purity and holiness should define what you wear!

In Matthew, Jesus draws a clear distinction between the clothing of a man of God and the clothing of a "soft man." The soft clothing that Jesus refers to is literally speaking of the type of clothing that isn't clearly masculine or feminine. It is the clothing of a homosexual.

In Proverbs, the same principle is applied relating to the clothing of "an harlot." The Bible is clear in these passages that different types of people dress differently. Men of God dress one way, homosexuals dress another, and wicked women dress yet another.

The first principle is this—your dress reveals your life character. How you dress always identifies you as a particular "kind" of person. This has always been the case and always will be. Your clothing makes an outward statement of what kind of person you are on the inside.

The second principle is this—your dress reveals your level of respect for yourself and others in a particular situation. What you wear shows your respect towards the following four things:

- Your respect for God
- Your respect for your environment
- Your respect for yourself as God's ambassador
- Your respect for others around you

Our culture believes in dress standards. Golf courses set standards for what players can wear on the course and in the clubhouse. Weddings and funerals usually cause us to dress more appropriately out of respect for those being honored or remembered. Special occasions like graduations, formal dinners, awards ceremonies, etc. all lean towards dressing better out of respect. Why should we honor or respect God any less than we would a deceased person or a couple getting married?

Your dress always reveals your character and your respect.

3. The Way You Dress Should Always Honor God

W *"For she had said unto the servant, What man is this that walketh in the field to meet us? And the servant had said, It is my master: therefore she took a vail, and covered herself."* —GENESIS 24:65

W *"She maketh herself coverings of tapestry; her clothing is silk and purple."*—PROVERBS 31:22

W *"For if the woman be not covered, let her also be shorn: but if it be a shame for a woman*

to be shorn or shaven, let her be covered."
—1 CORINTHIANS 11:6

M *"The life is more than meat, and the body is more than raiment."*—LUKE 12:23

"But ye are a chosen generation, a royal priesthood, an holy nation, a peculiar people; that ye should shew forth the praises of him who hath called you out of darkness into his marvellous light:"
—1 PETER 2:9

Since we see that your appearance is always a reflection of your heart, it makes sense that your clothing choices should be driven by a desire to please God, not by a desire to look like culture or be "in style."

There is nothing particularly wrong with being "in style"—it's not as if we are to deliberately try to be out of style; it is simply that our dress choices should not be driven by style first! When it comes to pleasing God or being in style, pleasing God should be our first commitment.

This principle prevents worldly brands, advertising, or pictures on clothing that would hurt the testimony of Christ. This also prevents dress that directly mimics the world's carnal trends (e.g., all black gothic; baggy, gangster-rap styles; rough-looking clothing, etc.).

4. The Way You Dress Should Be Appropriate to the Occasion

"The woman shall not wear that which pertaineth unto a man, neither shall a man put on a woman's garment: for all that do so are abomination unto the LORD thy God."—DEUTERONOMY 22:5

God is saying in this verse and in the verses we have already seen, to dress appropriately for your gender and your circumstances! There are clothing styles that are feminine and clothing styles that are masculine. Stay within bounds on your choices!

There are many different occasions where we may dress differently and we must strive to be appropriate.

At home: Be modest, be covered, and be appropriate across genders, even among family members. Be as appropriate with friends at home as you would in other public settings.

At church: Be more respectful to God than you would be at any other occasion. Think about when you might dress your best. Should God get your best? Remember, it is not about what God will accept—it is about what God deserves. It is about revealing a right heart of respect towards Him.

At school: Honor the standards and guidelines set up by your school authorities. This is basic submission and obedience, and God will bless you as you do so with a right spirit. As a side note, why would you dress better for class than for church? God deserves more honor than that.

At activities or in public: If God cares about what you wear, and if what you wear reveals your inward heart and character, as well as your outward identification—reconsider how you dress in public. Raise the standard. Be Christ's ambassador everywhere you go. Don't be ashamed to be a good ambassador for Christ.

At work: Honor those in authority at your workplace without compromising your standards as a Christian. If you take a job that requires you to dress less decently than you believe God desires, be willing to lose that job and allow God to provide you with another one.

At special events: Show respect for those hosting, those being honored, and those attending the event.

When we dress sloppy for church or other occasions, we're simply making this statement: "I care more about respecting my own whims than about respecting anyone else."

5. The Way You Dress Should Not Directly Identify with the World

"And it shall come to pass in that day, that the prophets shall be ashamed every one of his vision, when he hath prophesied; neither shall they wear a rough garment to deceive:"
—ZECHARIAH 13:4

"And it shall come to pass in the day of the LORD's sacrifice, that I will punish the princes, and the king's children, and all such as are clothed with strange apparel."—ZEPHANIAH 1:8

"For ye were sometimes darkness, but now are ye light in the Lord: walk as children of light:"
—EPHESIANS 5:8

The verse above in Zechariah talks about young men who belonged to God but were not willing to be identified with God—so they changed the way they dressed! They wanted to identify with the world.

The verse in Zephaniah refers to God punishing those who have turned away from Him. One of the ways He identifies them—or one of the telltale signs that they do not belong to Him, is that they are clothed in "strange apparel." The word *strange* speaks of a variety of degrees and applications from foreign to adulterous to outlandish.

The application of the above verses is clear. When I am loving God and living for Him, my dress will reveal it. When

I am following the world and am ashamed of God, my dress will reveal that as well. Too often Christians are caught up in following the entertainment industry trends—music, TV, movies, or in following sports or worldly heroes in their dress choices.

Does what you wear connect you more with the world or with Christ? Are you following style trends more than God? Are you more concerned with being "in style" than "in fellowship" with God? Are you willing to dress in a way that connects you to God's righteousness?

6. The Way You Dress Should Lead Others to Respect You More

"Then they went out to see what was done; and came to Jesus, and found the man, out of whom the devils were departed, sitting at the feet of Jesus, clothed, and in his right mind: and they were afraid."—LUKE 8:35

This passage shows the response of others to the change in one man's life. It is powerful to note that when he was possessed, he was unclothed, but when God saved him, he was clothed and in his right mind!

Man looks on the outward appearance—people immediately formulate a respect level towards you based on how you are dressed. These people were afraid because of the radical change in this man's life and because of the amazing power of Christ. Isn't it amazing how a clothed man changes people's perspective of a situation?!

When you learn how to dress appropriately and in honor to the Lord, everyone who comes into contact with you will respect you more! There is much respect to be gained in dressing right!

7. The Way You Dress Should Influence Others toward God

> *"...for man looketh on the outward appearance..."*—1 SAMUEL 16:7

> *"Let your light so shine before men, that they may see your good works, and glorify your Father which is in heaven."*—MATTHEW 5:16

> *"Teaching us that, denying ungodliness and worldly lusts, we should live soberly, righteously, and godly, in this present world;"*—TITUS 2:12

> *"Having your conversation honest among the Gentiles: that, whereas they speak against you as evildoers, they may by your good works, which they shall behold, glorify God in the day of visitation."*—1 PETER 2:12

Your appearance always influences others. They formulate their opinions of your God by how you look! This is just a fact of life. People judge your appearance, and they judge God *by* your appearance.

Do you value your good influence on others more than you value your right to "wear whatever you want"? Decide that in your choice of clothing, you will be a witness for Christ, not a witness for culture!

8. The Way You Dress Should Show Respect to Godly Authorities

"Obey them that have the rule over you, and submit yourselves: for they watch for your souls, as they that must give account, that they may do it with joy, and not with grief: for that is unprofitable for you."—HEBREWS 13:17

"Honour thy father and thy mother: that thy days may be long upon the land which the LORD thy God giveth thee."—EXODUS 20:12

"Honour thy father and mother; (which is the first commandment with promise;)" —EPHESIANS 6:2

"Servants, be obedient to them that are your masters according to the flesh, with fear and trembling, in singleness of your heart, as unto Christ;"—EPHESIANS 6:5

W *"For after this manner in the old time the holy women also, who trusted in God, adorned themselves, being in subjection unto their own husbands:"*—1 PETER 3:5

Adorn · verb · to put in proper order

Adorn means "to put in proper order;" the word picture is "putting out a wick." The principle here for ladies is that the "adorning" is to cover something very precious and holy that belongs to God and eventually to your husband. Your clothing should not "light a flame" in men; it should help to put it out. There's only one flame you should "light" with your clothing—your husband's.

Many times, especially for young people, our dress is determined by those in authority over us. This is true all the time with parents; much of the time with teachers, pastors, and employers; and some of the time at other places, like golf courses and restaurants. Unless these authorities are asking you to defy the direct commands of God, then these preferences ought to be honored and obeyed with a right spirit.

In other words, for a teenager and sometimes for adults, this is more of an obedience choice than a fashion choice! The issue for most people isn't "what is right in my opinion" but rather, "what is right according to those in authority over me."

For a woman, this authority will be your husband's! As you obey godly authorities now in your life, you're growing towards a right relationship in marriage!

Are you willing to honor your authorities in the way you dress? If so, be ready—God will bless that spirit! This right heart is what God is looking for!

9. The Way You Dress Should Encourage Growth in You and Others

"For at the window of my house I looked through my casement, And beheld among the simple ones, I discerned among the youths, a young man void of understanding, Passing through the street near her corner; and he went the way to her house, In the twilight, in the evening, in the black and dark night: And, behold, there met him a woman with the attire of an harlot,

and subtil of heart. (She is loud and stubborn; her feet abide not in her house: Now is she without, now in the streets, and lieth in wait at every corner.) So she caught him, and kissed him, and with an impudent face said unto him, I have peace offerings with me; this day have I payed my vows. Therefore came I forth to meet thee, diligently to seek thy face, and I have found thee. I have decked my bed with coverings of tapestry, with carved works, with fine linen of Egypt. I have perfumed my bed with myrrh, aloes, and cinnamon. Come, let us take our fill of love until the morning: let us solace ourselves with loves. For the goodman is not at home, he is gone a long journey: He hath taken a bag of money with him, and will come home at the day appointed. With her much fair speech she caused him to yield, with the flattering of her lips she forced him. He goeth after her straightway, as an ox goeth to the slaughter, or as a fool to the correction of the stocks;"—PROVERBS 7:6–22

The first principle is that your dress and your behavior are interrelated. Your dress reflects your behavior, and your behavior reflects your dress. This was the case with the woman in the "attire of an harlot." Even secular studies reveal that if you dress well, you do well—in school, in sports, at work, when studying, when reading, when walking with God, etc. Dress well for the activity in which you are seeking to grow!

The second principle is that your dress affects others and their growth. In this passage, a simple one was seduced by the immodest dress of a young woman! The way you dress will directly influence others around you—are you influencing them towards God or away?

Choose to dress in a way that encourages your spiritual growth and the spiritual growth of those around you!

10. The Way You Dress Always Reflects Your Level of Spiritual Maturity

> **W** *"Whose adorning let it not be that outward adorning of plaiting the hair, and of wearing of gold, or of putting on of apparel; But let it be the hidden man of the heart, in that which is not corruptible, even the ornament of a meek and quiet spirit, which is in the sight of God of great price."*—1 PETER 3:3–4

> *"When I was a child, I spake as a child, I understood as a child, I thought as a child: but when I became a man, I put away childish things."*—1 CORINTHIANS 13:11

The verses in 1 Peter speak directly to young ladies. Simply put, people who are completely taken up by how they look physically are focusing on the wrong parts of life! They are spiritually immature. Our first concern should be that our heart be right with God and then that our appearance be pleasing to God.

As you grow in maturity, your clothing will simply be one of many ways that you choose to "honor God" outwardly! Your dress is not a fashion statement, an identity crisis, or an attempt to gain popularity or acceptance; your dress is the outward revelation of your spiritual maturity, your heart for God, and your relationship with Him.

Conclusion

There is coming a day when God Himself will literally determine exactly what you wear for all of eternity. Submitting to Him now is merely preparation for honoring Him in eternity!

> *"And round about the throne were four and twenty seats: and upon the seats I saw four and twenty elders sitting, clothed in white raiment; and they had on their heads crowns of gold."*
> —REVELATION 4:4

As we close this chapter, consider this challenge:

> *"But put ye on the Lord Jesus Christ, and make not provision for the flesh, to fulfil the lusts thereof."*—ROMANS 13:14

May what you "put on" every day from this point forward be a true and right reflection of the Lord Jesus Christ. Submit your clothing choices to Him and let Him be honored first in your life!

Questions for Personal Study (Men)
Modesty and Appropriateness

1. Describe what changes in your dress would please the Lord. (Are you willing to make these changes?)

2. How would others judge or associate you if all they had to work with is your appearance?

3. Consider sorting through some clothes and getting rid of anything that would not honor the Lord.

4. Write out and memorize Romans 13:14 about "putting on Christ."

5. Pray right now and express a heart to submit to God and honor Him in your dress decisions.

Questions for Personal Study (Ladies)
Modesty and Appropriateness

1. Describe what changes in your dress would please the Lord. (Are you willing to make these changes?)

2. How would others judge or associate you if all they had to work with is your appearance?

3. Describe the different kinds of clothing that different types of women wear.

4. Consider sorting through some clothing to get rid of anything that would be too tight or immodest.

5. Write out and memorize Romans 13:14 about "putting on Christ."

6. Pray right now and express a heart to submit to God and to dress modestly and holily.

CHAPTER FIVE

Appropriate Conduct and Etiquette

Behaving in a Way that Honors Christ

[Charity] "Doth not behave itself unseemly, seeketh not her own, is not easily provoked, thinketh no evil;"—1 CORINTHIANS 13:5

Caveman Conduct

Have you ever wondered why culture is so infatuated with things that are "crude" or "edgy"? Whether it's foul language, references to bodily functions, or mis-treatment of others—it seems that the world laughs primarily at things that are from the gutter. Why is it that the louder you can burp, the more gross or tasteless you can be, or the more foul your mouth, the funnier and "cooler" you are in the eyes of others?

Even Christians often find themselves humored by the crude, the profane, the innuendo, and the ugly things in life. God profiles these people this way: *"Unto the pure all things are pure: but unto them that are defiled and unbelieving is nothing pure; but even their mind and conscience is defiled"*

(Titus 1:15). In other words, to some people, everything has a double meaning. Some people are consumed with gutter thoughts, gutter talk, and gutter friends.

As a Christian, you are living in a culture that is trying to pervert you. The world is trying to distort your thinking and ultimately change your character and heart. Satan is tricky, and he messes you up just a little at a time. One bad joke here, one thoughtless deed there, one wrong friend, one step into the gutter—little by little he wants to warp you. If he can, he would turn you into a spiritual Neanderthal—a mental caveman who cannot take life seriously.

The problem is, nobody really respects these kinds of people. They seem to walk around wearing a sign that says, "My mind is always in the gutter" or "I came from the shallow end of the gene pool!" They label themselves as goof-offs and people never take them seriously. When it comes time to really depend upon someone, count on someone, or tackle some serious matter—these are not the guys you would choose!

There is an entirely different breed of person on this planet. This kind of person is respected and highly revered. This kind of person is seen as a mature example, a leader, and a sharp individual. This kind of person knows what is appropriate and what isn't. This kind of person knows when to be serious and when to laugh. He knows what is right and what is wrong. He knows when to laugh and when to walk away.

You might call this person "well-mannered." You might say she is sharp in how she handles herself. You might say he understands how to behave in various situations and how to take life seriously. One thing is for sure—these are the people who are trusted and respected. These are the ones who get hired and promoted. These are the ones who get selected for responsibility and opportunities. These are the ones who God honors in life.

It's all about etiquette—manners—how we act in a variety of situations and circumstances. When you were a child, people didn't necessarily expect you to have this stuff down, but now they do! You're either an adult or an emerging adult, and others expect you to know what is appropriate.

Admittedly, there is a wide variety of preferences on the matters that we will study in this chapter. Some people have higher standards than others when it comes to manners. One thing is for sure, the better you understand these principles and apply them, the more mature and respected you will be in life.

These matters of manners have big implications for your future. This chapter is about far more than "not burping in your grandmother's face." If you approach this study with a teachable spirit and an open heart, your *whole life* will go better. It is that simple. You will get a job you wouldn't have gotten. You will be viewed by others as more mature. And you'll be envied by all the people who don't have a problem burping in grandma's face!

Not long ago, two men driving in Southern California got into a battle of road rage after one cut the other off in a parking lot. The hot-headed men sped out of the parking lot in a fit of anger, chasing, driving recklessly, dodging and weaving in and out of traffic. They endangered a lot of lives before finally one forced the other to careen out of control. The driver tried frantically to regain control, but in the process an innocent little girl on a nearby sidewalk was killed. A young life was taken simply because two men became needlessly angry at each other. What a pointless tragedy.

The self-control we will study in these pages has big implications. Learning how to behave could be a matter of life and death at some point in your future.

God has a lot to say about our manners and conduct, so let's get started! Ask God to make these good manners a part of your life starting today.

What God Says about Our Manners

[Charity] "Doth not behave itself unseemly, seeketh not her own, is not easily provoked, thinketh no evil;"—1 CORINTHIANS 13:5

The Word of God says much about our manners, or our behavior. Notice in our text that God says we should not "behave…unseemly." When we speak about our manners, we are really referring to the little details of our outward behavior.

Unseemly · adj. · uncomely, unbecoming, ugly; inappropriate

Notice what God says about our behavior in each of the verses below:

"Be of good courage, and let us behave ourselves valiantly for our people, and for the cities of our God: and let the LORD do that which is good in his sight."—1 CHRONICLES 19:13

"I will behave myself wisely in a perfect way. O when wilt thou come unto me? I will walk within my house with a perfect heart."—PSALM 101:2

"And the people shall be oppressed, every one by another, and every one by his neighbour: the child shall behave himself proudly

against the ancient, and the base against the honourable."—ISAIAH 3:5

Behave himself proudly · verb · act insolently (or with an aggressive lack of respect in speech or behavior)

These verses show us that our behavior can have two extremes. It can be valiant and perfect, or it can be proud and insolent. In our culture today, we see more proud, insolent manners than we do valiant and perfect-hearted manners. Notice this verse:

"God is my strength and power: and he maketh my way perfect."—2 SAMUEL 22:33

Way · noun · course of life or mode of action

Perfect · adj. · without blemish, sincere, undefiled

This verse is teaching that by God's power and strength, your lifestyle and direction will be sincere and without blemish or defect. Your manners will be wholesome and will reflect God's presence and power in your life.

The Bible also teaches that different manners are appropriate in different settings. Though there are many such examples, here is just one where God teaches us that our behavior or manners in "God's house" ought to be distinct from other settings.

"But if I tarry long, that thou mayest know how thou oughtest to behave thyself in the house of God..."—1 TIMOTHY 3:15

All of these verses show that the Bible makes a clear case for our manners. God gives us strong and clear instructions as to how we are to behave ourselves as His children.

Do you have a heart that desires to grow in understanding God's standard of behavior and manners? Let's learn some critical principles about developing a well-mannered life that is pleasing to the Lord.

1. Your Manners Are a Reflection of Your Heart

Though we've said this in previous chapters, it is vital that you bear in mind that your outward life as a Christian is merely a reflection of your inward heart for God. We ought never to merely conform our outward behavior to a standard for the sake of appearances. We must approach these principles from the heart! Change in our outward lives must flow from within first!

> *"And if thou wilt walk before me, as David thy father walked, in integrity of heart, and in uprightness, to do according to all that I have commanded thee, and wilt keep my statutes and my judgments:"*—1 KINGS 9:4

God made it clear in this verse that David's walk was a reflection of David's heart! Even so, your outward walk—your manners—always reflect your heart.

> *"A good man out of the good treasure of his heart bringeth forth that which is good; and an evil man out of the evil treasure of his heart bringeth forth that which is evil: for of the abundance of the heart his mouth speaketh."*—LUKE 6:45

2. Bad Manners Flow from Bad Relationships

"Be not deceived: evil communications corrupt good manners."—1 CORINTHIANS 15:33

"But were mingled among the heathen, and learned their works."—PSALM 106:35

"I have not sat with vain persons, neither will I go in with dissemblers."—PSALM 26:4

Vain · adj. · someone wrapped up in uselessness

Dissembler · noun · someone who hides or conceals things; someone who makes things secret

"Forsake the foolish, and live; and go in the way of understanding."—PROVERBS 9:6

We always become like the people we spend time with! In addition to this, others judge us by those with whom we spend time.

One of the most important choices you make as a young person is who you spend time with! This choice will literally shape your manners and your behavior. You will adapt your life, if only subconsciously, to those with whom you spend time.

If you desire a life that reflects good manners and godliness, you must turn away from relationships with vain, dissembling, and foolish people as defined above. You must choose to hang around people who will sharpen you, help you grow, and encourage a life of godliness.

3. Right Manners Flow from a Heart of Respect for God and Others

"Let us hear the conclusion of the whole matter: Fear God, and keep his commandments: for this is the whole duty of man."—ECCLESIASTES 12:13

"Be kindly affectioned one to another with brotherly love; in honour preferring one another;" —ROMANS 12:10

"If it be possible, as much as lieth in you, live peaceably with all men."—ROMANS 12:18

"Honour all men. Love the brotherhood. Fear God. Honour the king."—1 PETER 2:17

One major problem in today's culture is that people of all ages generally do not care how they behave. They have a total lack of respect for God and others. They lack a healthy "fear of God." As a result, they don't have a foundational consideration of "how to act" or "how to treat others."

What should cause you to desire to "act right"? Simply, a fear (or respect) of God and consideration of others. The above verses teach us to love one another, prefer one another, live peaceably with all men, honor all men, and fear God. These principles are the foundation of a well-mannered life.

Our manners reflect how much we respect God and men. We must recognize we do not have the "right" to behave how we want. We have a responsibility to behave how God wants! We should lay down our "rights" and willingly take up a desire to please Christ.

When you respect God and others, you will want your manners to reflect that respect.

4. The Manners of a Christian Will Be Distinctly Different than Those of a Non-Christian

"And ye shall know that I am the Lord: for ye have not walked in my statutes, neither executed my judgments, but have done after the manners of the heathen that are round about you."—EZEKIEL 11:12

"And be not conformed to this world: but be ye transformed by the renewing of your mind, that ye may prove what is that good, and acceptable, and perfect, will of God."—ROMANS 12:2

"Take heed to thyself that thou be not snared by following them, after that they be destroyed from before thee; and that thou enquire not after their gods, saying, How did these nations serve their gods? even so will I do likewise." —DEUTERONOMY 12:30

"Now therefore make confession unto the Lord God of your fathers, and do his pleasure: and separate yourselves from the people of the land, and from the strange wives."—EZRA 10:11

Throughout God's Word, He teaches us that our lifestyle as Christians will be different—separate from the world. You cannot have the Holy Spirit transforming you inside without it showing up in your manner of life.

Question—are you ashamed of being different for Christ? If so, you will quench all of the change that God desires to bring into your life. But you'll pay a very high price! We'll see in a moment that there are great rewards to having a life that pleases Christ above all. Decide that you will not be ashamed of God's presence and power in your life! Dare to be different. Consider Bible characters like Joseph, Daniel, and Joshua who all took a stand! God blessed them greatly for daring to trust Him and honor Him first!

Embrace being different for God! Be courageously separate for God! Be willing to let God shape your behavior so that you "stick out" a little bit! It will be well worth it!

5. God's Word Is Filled with Instruction about Our "Manner of Life"

"But thou hast fully known my doctrine, manner of life, purpose, faith, longsuffering, charity, patience,"—2 TIMOTHY 3:10

"But as he which hath called you is holy, so be ye holy in all manner of conversation;" —1 PETER 1:15

"Seeing then that all these things shall be dissolved, what manner of persons ought ye to be in all holy conversation and godliness."—2 PETER 3:11

"A bishop then must be blameless, the husband of one wife, vigilant, sober, of good behaviour, given to hospitality, apt to teach;"—1 TIMOTHY 3:2

"The aged women likewise, that they be in behaviour as becometh holiness, not false accusers, not given to much wine, teachers of good things;"—TITUS 2:3

Notice in each of these verses that God references our "manner of life," our "conversation," our "manner of persons," "good behavior," and "behavior that becometh holiness."

It is clear that there are two ways to live—one way that defies holiness and godliness, and one way that becomes it! While many so-called Christians today believe that they have freedom to live however they desire, the Bible does not give us this kind of freedom. This reckless lifestyle is actually a great abuse of the freedom and grace that we have in Christ.

The message from God to you is that the way you behave matters! God is very concerned that you live in a manner that honors Him. Let's see how this life is produced.

6. God's Word and His Holy Spirit Will Produce a Well-Mannered Life

"The law of the LORD is perfect, converting the soul: the testimony of the LORD is sure, making wise the simple. The statutes of the LORD are right, rejoicing the heart: the commandment of the LORD is pure, enlightening the eyes. The fear of the LORD is clean, enduring for ever: the judgments of the LORD are true and righteous altogether. More to be desired are they than gold, yea, than much fine gold: sweeter also than honey and the honeycomb. Moreover by them is thy servant warned: and in keeping of them there is great reward."—PSALM 19:7–11

"Therefore if any man be in Christ, he is a new creature: old things are passed away; behold, all things are become new."—2 CORINTHIANS 5:17

Fortunately, producing a godly life or a well-mannered life is not left up to us! Frankly, it would be very difficult to remember all the small instructions of God and to act upon every one of them every day! It would be impossible.

So God promises us that the work is up to Him! This is the BEST part of this study. If you will simply surrender your will to God, He will do the work! He will produce a life of good manners by His power! We will see this again in a moment in the life of Jesus.

Will you allow God's Word and God's Spirit to change your lifestyle? It begins by simply having a heart attitude that says, "Lord, I know that I am not my own and my behavior is a reflection of You. I surrender my 'right' to live how I want, and I ask You to produce a lifestyle that pleases You."

7. A Well-Mannered Life Is a Reflection of the New Man Within

> *"This I say therefore, and testify in the Lord, that ye henceforth walk not as other Gentiles walk, in the vanity of their mind, Having the understanding darkened, being alienated from the life of God through the ignorance that is in them, because of the blindness of their heart: Who being past feeling have given themselves over unto lasciviousness, to work all uncleanness with greediness. But ye have not so learned Christ; If so be that ye have heard him, and have been taught by him, as the truth is in Jesus: That ye put off concerning the former conversation the old man, which is corrupt according to the deceitful lusts; And be renewed in the spirit of your mind; And that ye put on the new man, which after God is created in righteousness and true holiness."*
> —Ephesians 4:17–24

> *"But now ye also put off all these; anger, wrath, malice, blasphemy, filthy communication out of*

your mouth. Lie not one to another, seeing that ye have put off the old man with his deeds; And have put on the new man, which is renewed in knowledge after the image of him that created him:"—COLOSSIANS 3:8–10

Since godly manners don't develop naturally, when you live a well-mannered life, you are showing God's work in your heart!

How would anybody ever know that you are a Christian if they couldn't tell by the way you live and act? It is God's desire that your inner man shows up in your outward life!

8. A Well-Mannered Life Helps Avoid the Appearance of Evil

"Abstain from all appearance of evil."
—1 THESSALONIANS 5:22

One of the best reasons to have godly manners is so that people will not misjudge you. It is so easy to be misunderstood or misjudged by others. It is not always fair, but it is a reality! The more you seek to avoid the appearance of evil, the less you will be misunderstood.

Godly manners will cause you to live "above reproach," and will help you guard your testimony as a Christian.

9. A Well-Mannered Life Was Modeled by Jesus

"And Jesus increased in wisdom and stature, and in favour with God and man."—LUKE 2:52

As we consider this verse, first think about these definitions of Bible words:

Increased · verb · to drive forward or advance by force; to grow

This was a decision to intentionally grow!

Stature · noun · growth in maturity as well as age and size

Favour · noun · graciousness in manner of acting, especially the divine influence upon the heart and its reflection in the life

This verse is literally saying that Jesus chose to deliberately grow to maturity. As He did, His manners and His lifestyle became more gracious as a result of God's work in His heart! Amazing!

God's influence in the heart of Jesus is what caused Him to grow in godly manners and lifestyle—favour!

In other words, your godly manners will directly relate to your relationship with God! As you grow closer to Him, He will produce a life of favour.

10. A Well-Mannered Life Brings the Favour of God and Men

"Let not mercy and truth forsake thee: bind them about thy neck; write them upon the table of thine heart: So shalt thou find favour and good understanding in the sight of God and man."—Proverbs 3:3–4

This verse says that mercy and truth should be in our hearts and around our necks! That's both inward and outward! In other words, when we choose to live godly we will find favour and understanding from both God and men!

This is the reward of godly manners! Everyone wants favour! Everyone wants to be truly understood by others, respected by others, and favoured by God and others.

Simply, a well-mannered life will give you the respect of God and men! You will be chosen before others for a better job, a better position, a better paycheck, and a better life! Good manners are well worth the trouble!

Be careful that this isn't your first motivation. We must choose to live a well-mannered life because it honors Christ, but the fringe benefit is that God honors us in return!

Conclusion

We've seen the biblical principles that should compel us to live godly and to behave wisely. The following pages present a list that highlights "good manners" and appropriate etiquette.

Take a moment and read this list with a willing heart and soft spirit. Ask the Lord to make this list a reality in your life! Whether you understand each point or not, seek to honor the Lord and to bring your manner of life in line with a high standard of Christian etiquette.

Remember, above all, right etiquette should be a product of a right heart!

Questions for Personal Study
Appropriate Conduct and Etiquette

1. Read the etiquette list and highlight things that you learn and will work on.

2. What point was the most convicting to you in this study?

3. Describe the reasons God is so concerned about our manners or behavior.

4. As you read the etiquette list, what are your strengths or the areas in which you are doing well?

5. Write out and memorize Luke 2:52 about increasing in "favour."

6. Pray right now and express a heart to submit to God and honor Him in your personal etiquette.

Basic Rules of Etiquette
At School and in the Classroom
Do

- Be on time (punctual).
- Acknowledge and greet every faculty and staff member you see.
- Dress according to school standards.
- Keep your locker and desk area clean and organized.
- Respond to reprimands in sincerity with an apology.
- Remember to take the right books and tools to class.
- Turn in homework and projects on time and do your best work.
- Follow the class rules with a willing heart.
- Follow common table manners in the lunchroom.

Don't

- Don't ridicule other students publicly or privately.
- Don't talk disrespectfully to a teacher or about a teacher.
- Don't contradict or argue with a teacher, especially in front of others.
- Don't disturb others by making obnoxious noises (e.g., clicking pen, tapping foot, etc.).

In Church and Whenever the Bible Is Opened
Do

- Dress appropriately in respect.
- Acknowledge and greet church members.
- Turn your cell phone off or put it on "silent."
- Introduce yourself to visitors and new people.
- Have your Bible with you for all classes and services.

- Follow along in your Bible when Scripture is being read.
- Share your Bible with the person next to you if needed.
- Face the people seated as you make your way down the pew.
- Focus on the speaker and give your undivided attention.
- Sit up straight in your chair or pew.
- Remember, your actions reflect your respect for God and His Word.
- Sing along with the congregation.
- Thank the preacher or teacher when the lesson helped you.
- Learn the discipline of staying awake.
- Men—Allow ladies to enter the pew before you do.
- Men—Exit the pew to let a lady enter if you are seated at the end.
- Men—Give a sincere "amen" when appropriate.

Don't
- Don't be late.
- Don't chew gum, eat food, or drink a beverage.
- Don't walk quickly or run down the aisles.
- Don't whisper or laugh under your breath during the service.
- Don't distract others around you.
- Don't look at your watch or a clock during the service.
- Don't sit in the back of the room when closer seats are available.
- Don't fan yourself.
- Don't walk out of the service, unless it is an emergency.
- Don't slouch in your seat or stare at the floor.

With the Opposite Gender and in Dating Relationships

Do

- Keep your conversation and words appropriate and respectful.
- Focus your attention on being polite and respectful.
- Men—Open the door for a lady.
- Men—Offer help when you see it is needed.
- Men—Offer your seat to a lady.
- Men—Always acknowledge and greet a girl's parents.
- Men—Look a girl in the eyes.
- Men—Offer your umbrella to a lady if it is raining.
- Men—Offer your suit jacket to a girl if it is cold.
- Men—Open a lady's car door and wait there until she is seated.
- Men—When a lady drops something, help her pick it up.
- Men—Walk on the outside of the sidewalk when with a lady.
- Men—Only shake hands if a lady extends her hand first.
- Men—Ask a girl's father for permission before writing or calling her.
- Men—Respect your parents' and her parents' wishes in every area.
- Ladies—Maintain a meek and quiet spirit.
- Ladies—Maintain a godly presence in physical posture and dress.
- Ladies—Seek your parents' approval before responding to a guy.

Don't

- Men—Don't let a lady carry boxes or large items.

- Men—Don't touch a lady, unless to help her recover from a fall.
- Men—Don't walk behind a lady on the stairway.
- Men—Don't spend time with a girl without her dad's permission.
- Ladies—Don't call or text guys on the phone.
- Ladies—Don't order the most expensive item on the menu.
- Ladies—Don't try to be the center of attention.
- Ladies—Don't touch guys, even jokingly.
- Ladies—Don't be forward or flirtatious.

Friends and Social Gatherings

Do

- Let people formulate their own opinions of others.
- Speak positively of people who are not present.
- Think before you speak.
- Refrain from bodily noises.
- Thank the host of a function.
- Make eye contact with others when talking.
- Show genuine interest in what others are saying.
- Learn how to ask questions and carry on conversation.
- Invite others "on the sidelines" to be involved socially.
- Politely introduce your friends and family to others.
- Defer the flow of conversation to elders or to those in authority.
- Stand straight, sit up straight, and focus your attention on others.
- Graciously accept compliments and defer praise to God and others.
- Men—Give a firm handshake to other men. (No dead fish!)

Don't

- Don't give attention to one person when others are around.
- Don't lose your temper or raise your voice.
- Don't discuss your break-ups with everyone.
- Don't talk badly about your spouse, family, or parents.
- Don't point out other people's bad manners.
- Don't brag about yourself.
- Don't whine and complain.
- Don't joke racially.
- Don't tell jokes that may embarrass people.
- Don't mock people for things they would not laugh at themselves.
- Don't mock people for something they cannot change.
- Don't monopolize or dominate a conversation.
- Don't gossip or conjecture about others.
- Men—Don't joke or talk inappropriately about ladies.
- Men—Don't participate with inappropriate talk or joking.
- Ladies—Don't ask the question, "Does this make me look fat?"

Cell Phones and Phone Calls

Do

- Turn your phone off when in church, restaurants, meetings, etc.
- Immediately give your name and greet the person.
- Be polite and speak clearly.
- Say "excuse me" when interrupting a conversation to take a call.
- End a call before trying to communicate with someone else.

- Respect other people's time.
- Take responsibility to end a conversation if you started it.

Don't
- Don't talk loudly in public places.
- Don't take calls at the table or in a restaurant.
- Don't take calls while you are talking with someone, if possible.
- Don't say anything inappropriate over the phone or in a text.
- Don't call early, late, or at "dinner time," unless it is an emergency.
- Men—Don't call, text, or email a girl without her dad's permission.
- Ladies—Don't call, text, or email guys.
- Ladies—Don't accept calls from guys without parental permission.

Everyday Speech and Conversation

Do
- Be gracious by using words like "please," "thank you," and "excuse me."
- Respond to authority with "yes, sir" and "no, ma'am."
- Use your speech to encourage and edify others.

Don't
- Don't be afraid to say "I'm sorry, will you forgive me?"
- Don't respond in sarcasm to a serious question.
- Don't use slang terms or gangster language.
- Don't use euphemisms—words used in place of offensive words (dang, darn it, jeez, frickin', freakin', gosh, golly, heck, etc.).

Table Manners

Do

- Use eating utensils appropriately.
- Place your napkin properly on your lap after being seated.
- Wait until everyone has their food before you start eating.
- Chew with your mouth closed.
- Offer the last of the food to others before taking it for yourself.
- Say "thank you" to the host (for young people, this includes your parents).
- Compliment the meal and the cook.
- Be pleasant in conduct or conversation.
- Place your spoon in your saucer if you want more tea or coffee.
- Break your bread; do not cut it.
- Use a napkin only for your mouth (not nose, face, or forehead).
- Eat slowly and converse with others.
- Politely ask someone to pass the dish you would like.
- Put down your knife after cutting and before eating.
- Men—Help a lady with her chair if she will be seated next to you.

Don't

- Don't sit until your host is seated.
- Don't reach across someone.
- Don't talk with your mouth full.
- Don't put your elbows on the table.
- Don't play with utensils or food.
- Don't sit too far back or slouch.
- Don't talk loudly or boisterously.
- Don't tilt your chair back.

- Don't make noises while eating.
- Don't indicate if you notice something unpleasant in the food.
- Don't leave the table before others, unless you ask to be excused.
- Don't draw attention when removing hair or items from food.
- Don't discuss things that might cause others to lose their appetite.
- Don't pick your teeth at the table; if you must, cover your mouth.
- Don't burp out loud.
- Don't take generous servings that would deplete a dish before everyone has been served.

Restaurants, Hotels and Public Places

Do

- Follow all table manners at restaurants.
- Stay to the right when walking in public places.
- Open the door for a person entering behind you.
- Be conscious of your voice level.
- Tip well (15% minimum) and discreetly.
- Pay the bill if you invited someone to lunch or dinner.
- Be friendly and respectful to the person helping you.
- Graciously accept when someone offers to pay the bill.
- Leave a generous tip with a Gospel tract.

Don't

- Don't talk on a cell phone when someone is taking your order.
- Don't be late if you have reservations.
- Don't point or stare at other people.

- Don't spit, loudly clear your throat, or loudly blow your nose.
- Don't touch food that you do not plan to eat.

Workplace or Other Professional Environments

Do

- Be punctual for work.
- Keep your workspace clean and organized.
- Follow the guidelines for dress.
- Follow your company's policies and procedures.
- Be friendly and polite towards other employees and customers.
- Converse respectfully with employers and managers.
- Respect and serve all customers efficiently and graciously.
- Work hard and give your best effort in every area.
- Stay focused on your work.
- Maintain your Christian testimony.

Don't

- Don't disturb other employees with distractions, questions, etc.
- Don't talk excessively with other employees during work hours.
- Don't do personal things while "on the clock."
- Don't use company equipment for personal use without permission.
- Don't witness "on the clock"—look for break times, etc.
- Don't participate in inappropriate jokes and behavior.

When with Guests and New Acquaintances

Do

- Stand when a visitor or guest walks into the room.
- Introduce yourself and shake the guest's hand when appropriate.
- Learn and practice polite small talk.
- Introduce someone by telling their name and your relationship.

Don't

- Men—Don't take off your tie when you are with company, out of respect.
- Don't ask questions that might make a guest uncomfortable.

In Front of an Audience

Do

- Stand up straight with your hands to your sides or in front.
- Hold your head straight up.
- Dress sharp and look well groomed.
- Focus intently on the speaker and follow him with your eyes.
- Nod in agreement or say "amen" when appropriate.
- Speak clearly and slowly—project your voice.
- Stand when a lady approaches.

Don't

- Don't rock back and forth or sway from side to side.
- Don't put your hands in your pockets.
- Don't do repetitive, nervous actions.
- Don't cross your legs on a platform.

- Don't chew gum.
- Don't hold a microphone too low.
- Don't mumble or use a lot of fillers (um, like, uh, you know…).
- Don't stare at the audience when another is speaking.

Parents and Authority

Do

- Be respectful, obedient, and give honor.
- Maintain eye contact and listen intently when being spoken to.
- Respect authority with your posture and your facial expressions.
- Prefer and serve authority with a sincere heart.
- Show initiative with chores and acts of kindness.
- Express thankfulness constantly.

Don't

- Don't laugh or mumble under your breath.
- Don't leave the room or walk away when being spoken to.
- Don't withdraw from family relationships.
- Don't heave or sigh.
- Don't roll your eyes.
- Don't participate in dishonoring treatment of authority.

Letters, Notes, and Emails

Do

- Send handwritten thank you notes for any gifts or acts of kindness.

- In a thank you note...
  - Greet the giver (Dear <Name>).
  - Express your gratitude (Thank you for...).
  - State how you will use what they have given you.
  - Refer to the past and mention the future (It was great to...and I hope to...).
  - Thank them again (Thanks again for...).
  - Regards (Sincerely)
  - Make thank you letters about them, not about you.
- Use blue or black ink in formal writing.
- Write legibly and use correct grammar and structure.
- Refrain from typing personal notes if possible.

Don't

- Don't use a hard-to-read font or color.
- Don't state the obvious (e.g., "I am just writing to say").
- Don't directly mention money but rather thank them for their generosity or kindness.
- Don't lie about liking a gift, instead compliment the thoughtfulness/generosity of the giver.
- Don't type emails in all caps—this is like yelling.
- Don't gossip in notes and emails.

Weddings and Funerals

Do

- Make small talk with other guests at a wedding.
- Dress appropriately.
- Keep a quiet, respectful, proper, and sober spirit.
- Congratulate the bride and groom and their families.
- Express condolences to the family of the deceased.
- Take a gift or card.

- Sign the guest book.

Don't

- Don't chew gum or call attention to yourself.
- Ladies—Don't wear white to a wedding.

General/Other

Do

- Make sure your shoes are always clean and polished.
- Stand when someone in authority enters a room.
- Stand to greet someone who approaches your table.
- Use names (people like to hear their own name).
- If you don't know a name, introduce yourself.
- When hearing a new name, try to use it right away.
- Cover your mouth to cough and excuse yourself if necessary.
- Cover your mouth with a tissue or napkin when sneezing.
- Stand and sit up straight—posture and body language speak loudly.
- Keep your mouth closed when you are not talking.
- Men—Stand when a lady enters the room.
- Men—Shake hands firmly and make eye contact.

Don't

- Don't pick anything—nose, ears, teeth, fingernails.
- Don't ask dating couples when they're getting married.
- Don't ask married couples when they're planning to have children.
- Don't ask a woman when her baby is due.
- Ladies—Don't wear things that accentuate your body inappropriately.

CHAPTER SIX

Personal Appearance and Hygiene

Honoring Christ in My Body

"For ye are bought with a price: therefore glorify God in your body, and in your spirit, which are God's."—1 CORINTHIANS 6:20

Teenage Mutants

"Who rode their bicycle through your mouth?!"—Those were the first rather hurtful words I heard at Wednesday night Bible study when I arrived at church with my new "head-gear"! As if braces and a retainer weren't enough torture, my orthodontist had to wire an erector set to my jaw! And even worse, he then made me wear it—IN PUBLIC! What a devastating thing it is to walk around with a hamster-sized ferris-wheel strapped to your face!

Then I remember the day I was asked if I was wearing "water skis" for tennis shoes. I was in seventh grade, and my feet had grown faster than the rest of my body, giving me that really cool "Ronald-McDonald-foot" look! If I had painted them red, people would have been asking me for autographs!

Then there was the "shrimp factor"! In Junior High I was really rinky-dink sized! I think I was all of five feet two inches, while every girl in my class was nearing six feet! Why did I have to go to school with the "Amazons"? I was the smallest guy in the youth group—I couldn't even serve the volleyball over the net on a regular-sized court. My legs were so skinny that people called me "chicken-legs," and I weighed ninety pounds dripping wet and bench pressed the same! Identity crisis doesn't even begin to describe it. I didn't think I would make it through those terrible times!

Two years later, I was five-nine, weighed 150 pounds, bench pressed 220 pounds, quarterbacked my JV football team, and actually went to school with girls smaller than I was. I went from being the kid everybody loved to tease to being somewhat normal, but getting there sure was difficult!

Have you noticed, since you became a teenager, how much your body has changed? Depending upon your age, there's a lot happening to you physically right now. I remember being a teenager and at times, feeling like a freak of nature! You're changing more than you realize! There's a ton of reconstructing going on in your body and it leads to a lot of problems—at least in the short term.

Your brain is rewiring itself, so you often feel confused, frustrated, and lost. (And culture is only making matters worse by throwing so much sin at you during this mentally unstable time.)

Your body is using every bit of energy it can to produce growth and physical change, which means you often get really, really tired very suddenly. There are probably times you feel like you could sleep for a year and still wake up tired! And frankly, there are times when what you need most is a really long night's sleep—I'm talking 'til noon!

Your physical growth also means you feel awkward, your clothes don't always fit right, and you struggle at certain ages to be coordinated in sports and other things. You also have to deal with growing pains, a huge appetite, and a short emotional fuse.

Your physical changes mean that you're dealing with new smells, zits, and appearance issues—like bad hair days! New desires show up—ones that you will struggle with guarding and restraining until marriage. And every day you are at risk of being made fun of for something you cannot control—your complexion, your weight, your physical proportions, or that second head that's growing out of your neck.

Your schedule has changed and not everyone gets it! Elementary school seems like cake! How you long for the day when school had recess and there was no such thing as "Chemistry"! Your day runs from early in the morning to late in the evening with very little down time—from class to class to sports practice to music lessons to homework to studying to bed! This would make anybody half crazy—and just being a teenager makes you half crazy to begin with—which means, now you are completely crazy!

It is definitely not easy being a teenager! In fact, I think I'd rather lose an arm than do that again. Don't get me wrong. I enjoyed being a teenager, but getting through it was sure tough at times.

In this study, we are going to examine some of the physical and emotional changes that have entered your life, and we will find out how to respond to them. The fact is, there are some new habits you're going to have to develop—like popping zits! As your body changes, God wants you to take better care of it. If you learn this stuff, you'll have fewer zits and more friends. If you don't—well let's just say your "personal zone" will get a lot bigger because people won't be able to stand the smell.

Let's find out what God says about taking care of your changing body!

Glorifying God in Our Bodies

In previous chapters, we've laid the foundation that God cares intimately about our outward appearance—including our clothing choices, our standards of modesty, our level of respect for God and others. God desires for our outward lifestyle to be "becoming of the Gospel of Christ," and He desires for a sincere heart of faith to show in our lifestyle.

In our last chapter, we focused on manners—or our outward behavior. In this study, we are going to focus on caring for and maintaining a healthy, clean, and sharp external life.

This chapter's text teaches us that we are to "glorify" God in our bodies! This word *glorify* literally means that we are to show God's character in our body! Amazing! Think about it. This is saying that you can either glorify or "not glorify" God in your physical presence—the clothes you wear, your hairstyle, your cleanliness, your physical appearance!

The Bible affirms that God cares about our bodies in these verses:

> "*I speak after the manner of men because of the infirmity of your flesh: for as ye have yielded your members servants to uncleanness and to iniquity unto iniquity; even so now yield your members servants to righteousness unto holiness.*"
> —ROMANS 6:19

> "*I beseech you therefore, brethren, by the mercies of God, that ye present your bodies a living*

sacrifice, holy, acceptable unto God, which is your reasonable service."—ROMANS 12:1

"*According to my earnest expectation and my hope, that in nothing I shall be ashamed, but that with all boldness, as always, so now also Christ shall be magnified in my body, whether it be by life, or by death.*"—PHILIPPIANS 1:20

"*And the very God of peace sanctify you wholly; and I pray God your whole spirit and soul and body be preserved blameless unto the coming of our Lord Jesus Christ.*"—1 THESSALONIANS 5:23

"*For we must all appear before the judgment seat of Christ; that every one may receive the things done in his body, according to that he hath done, whether it be good or bad.*"—2 CORINTHIANS 5:10

Let's examine some governing principles, and learn some practical ways that we can truly "glorify God" in our bodies.

1. A Godly Appearance Honors the Testimony of Christ

"*But ye are a chosen generation, a royal priesthood, an holy nation, a peculiar people; that ye should shew forth the praises of him who hath called you out of darkness into his marvellous light:*" —1 PETER 2:9

God says in this verse that we are to "shew forth" the praises of Christ! Having the right appearance can bring glory to God.

2. A Godly Appearance Cares for the "Temple of the Holy Spirit"

> *"What? know ye not that your body is the temple of the Holy Ghost which is in you, which ye have of God, and ye are not your own? For ye are bought with a price: therefore glorify God in your body, and in your spirit, which are God's."*—1 CORINTHIANS 6:19–20

When you were saved, the Holy Spirit of God came into your life and took up residence in you! This means that your body is the temple (or dwelling place) of God. How you care for your body is a reflection of your love for God and your understanding of His presence in your life!

Your earthly body is a gift from God, and He expects you to consider it as you would any other stewardship. Without it, you're dead! So learn to take care of it and learn to maintain it in a way that honors God.

3. The Need for Personal Cleanliness Changes during Teen Years

From about the time you turned twelve until you enter your early twenties, your body undergoes many changes and transitions. This happens to everybody, and there is no way to avoid it! It is the way God designed us.

Here are just a few of the physical changes we face during these years:

- Increased perspiration and body odor
- Increased body hair (facial, armpits, etc.)
- Muscle tone and physical shape changes.
- Feet grow first, then the body catches up.

- Rapid body growth results in bodily awkwardness.
- Usually girls grow faster than boys.
- Adult hormones and sexual desires begin to develop.
- Body fat is burned faster (more true in boys).
- Periods of high energy followed by exhaustion are common.
- Increased body oils result in complexion problems.
- Brain matter is being completely redeveloped.

All of these changes and others result in the need to change and increase your habits of daily hygiene and personal care. Simply put, you are not a child anymore. You now have an adult body that needs a bit more care and preparation than your childhood body did.

This daily care is not only normal and expected—it is a spiritual discipline. Caring well for your body is a practice that honors Christ.

4. Honoring God in My Body Begins with Daily Hygiene

Caring for your body in a way that honors God involves some daily personal disciplines. Practically speaking, this means you're going to have to wake up earlier, and you'll have to change some of your morning and evening routines.

There are many things that every young person should do daily, or multiple times per day:

- Shower every morning or evening (and after sports and work).
- Brush teeth well every morning and evening (or after every meal).
- Floss teeth at least once a day.

- Put on antiperspirant/deodorant every morning (not just deodorant).
- Shave well every day (starting from approximately eighth–tenth grade).
- Wash your face in evenings (hot water, soap, cleansing pads, etc.).
- Use medication on pimples (as needed).
- Wash hands (after shaking hands, working, touching pets, etc.).

5. Honoring God in My Body Includes Caring for My Body

In addition to daily routines of body care, there are things you should set aside time to do on a regular basis to maintain a clean, sharp, and well-kept testimony.

Here are some things you should do regularly:

- Clip your nails (both hands and feet).
- Keep your hair cut or trimmed (boys).
- Shave at least once a week (seventh–ninth grade boys).

In addition to this, there are several things you can do to care better for your complexion:

- Eat less sugar, especially chocolate.
- Drink less or no caffeine.
- Don't touch your face with your hands.
- Keep your hands and face clean (multiple times daily, clean face of body oils).
- Drink more water, more frequently.

6. Honoring God in My Body Includes Caring for My Clothing

We have already discussed principles of modesty in another chapter, but within the bounds of modesty, there are many clothing choices that impact your testimony for Christ and your outward appearance. Here are some general guidelines for men and women regarding your clothing and caring for your wardrobe.

Young Men

+ Iron your shirts and pants (except casual attire).
+ Polish your shoes regularly.
+ Always match your belt to your shoes.
+ Always match your socks to your pants.
+ Generally, don't mix two plaids or striped patterns (shirts and ties, etc.).
+ Tuck your shirt in except in highly casual settings.
+ Understand the difference between dress, casual, and play shoes.
+ Understand the difference between dress, casual, and play clothes.
+ Take good care of dry-clean-only clothes (keep hung up, etc.).
+ Always wear undershirts with dress shirts.
+ Choose masculine clothing styles.

Young Ladies

+ Iron your skirts and tops (except casual attire).
+ Polish shoes that require it (removing scuffs, etc.).
+ Make sure your shoes and purse coordinate with your outfit.

- Understand appropriate settings for nylons.
- Understand the difference between dress, casual, and play shoes.
- Understand the difference between dress, casual, and play clothes.
- Don't mix casual and dress styles (shoes, clothes, etc.).
- Take good care of dry-clean-only clothes (keep hung up, etc.).
- Don't over-accessorize (big jewelry, etc.—be tastefully conservative) (accessories should accent not dominate!).
- Choose feminine clothing styles.

7. Honoring God in My Body Includes a Right Hairstyle

"But the very hairs of your head are all numbered."—MATTHEW 10:30

"Doth not even nature itself teach you, that, if a man have long hair, it is a shame unto him? But if a woman have long hair, it is a glory to her: for her hair is given her for a covering."
—1 CORINTHIANS 11:14–15

"And they had hair as the hair of women"
—REVELATION 9:8

Young Men

- Submit your hairstyle to the Lord (a young man's hair is a reflection of his heart!).

- Keep it cut regularly (off collar and above ear).
- Style it with order (the world's style is disorder!).
- Choose a style that doesn't reflect the world.
- Choose a masculine style.
- Consider using gel or mousse to hold it in place if needed.

Young Ladies

- Submit your style choices to the Lord and your parents.
- Wash your hair regularly to keep it clean.
- Have it trimmed regularly to avoid split ends, etc.
- Use hair care products that keep it healthy.
- Choose a style that does not mimic the world (radiate godliness).
- When coloring hair, choose natural shades.
- Have a hairstyle that reflects order, not worldliness.
- Choose a feminine hairstyle.
- Choose a style that is appropriate for your age.
- Don't cover your eyes or face (don't hide behind your hair).

Additional Makeup Tips for Young Ladies

- Go with your parents' guidance, and do not resist their wisdom.
- Use the right amount of makeup (too much looks worldly).
- Highlight eyes, don't hide them (too much eye makeup looks worldly).
- Use a foundation color that matches your skin (not darker or lighter).

- Understand what colors look best with your skin tone.
- Use natural colors, not wild, dark, or weird colors (including lips and nails).

8. Honoring God in My Body Requires Personal Discipline

"But I keep under my body, and bring it into subjection: lest that by any means, when I have preached to others, I myself should be a castaway."—1 CORINTHIANS 9:27

The bottom line is that you must grow in maturity and step up to new responsibilities of caring for your appearance. This will require some new daily and weekly disciplines that you've never had before. But the rewards of looking and dressing sharp are many!

As you care for your appearance, you are honoring God, respecting others, and caring for the temple of the Holy Spirit!

Learn to adjust your daily routine and to discipline yourself to take good care of your body for the glory of God.

Conclusion

"I will praise thee; for I am fearfully and wonderfully made: marvellous are thy works; and that my soul knoweth right well."—PSALM 139:14

God has given you a body, and He is pleased when you take good care of it. Decide now that you will be a good steward of the growing body that God has given to you!

Questions for Personal Study
Personal Appearance and Hygiene

1. List and describe the ways that your life has changed in recent years.

2. Of all the points in this lesson, which one is God speaking to you the most about and why?

3. What do you think God means when He says we are to possess our "vessel" in "honour"?

4. List a few ways you could take better care of your "vessel" to honor the Lord.

5. Write out and memorize 1 Corinthians 6:20 about glorifying God in your body.

CHAPTER SEVEN

Biblical Authority

Accepting God's Plan for Authority in My Life

"Remember them which have the rule over you, who have spoken unto you the word of God: whose faith follow, considering the end of their conversation."—HEBREWS 13:7

"Obey them that have the rule over you, and submit yourselves: for they watch for your souls, as they that must give account, that they may do it with joy, and not with grief: for that is unprofitable for you."—HEBREWS 13:17

"Let every soul be subject unto the higher powers. For there is no power but of God: the powers that be are ordained of God."—ROMANS 13:1

On Second Thought...Stay on My Case!

It seems that the cry of the youth culture today is, "Get off my case!" In fact, not long ago, I asked a group of teenagers, "How many of you feel like someone is always on your case about something, and you wonder if you can get anything right?" To my amazement, every hand went up!

I realize that, if you're a young person, you probably feel that a lot of people are always telling you what to do. I realize you probably feel like you sometimes fail more than you succeed. But there is a bigger concern than merely "who's on your case."

There is a far darker cry and more sinister and dangerous movement among this generation. It is the "question authority" movement. It is the "parents are stupid and God doesn't exist" movement. There is a large segment of our culture that would teach you and lead you as far away from authority as possible. They would have you believe that God is a fable and authorities are the source of the problems in your life. They would encourage you to do what you want, when you want, however you want.

This type of thinking claims to offer you your individuality. It claims to give you freedom from the oppressive restraints of the adults in your life. But this thinking leads to a place you don't want to go—I promise. It leads to destruction—to a total loss of blessing and good potential. It leads to massive life-altering mistakes and destructive patterns that are in some ways irreversible.

Let me ask you a question: would you like to avoid the "train-wrecks" in life? Would you like to avoid personal disaster on many different levels in your future? If so, then this chapter more than any other in this study, can place you on the path of "regret-proof" living. The things we are about to study will place you in the direct path of God's oncoming blessings and will protect you from a life of heartaches and missteps.

Do you believe that God has good plans for you? Do you believe that He has blessings and opportunities in store for you that you haven't even imagined? He certainly does, and He has a process of giving you those blessings. He has a path of leading you into those blessings. They won't come to you randomly, but rather in a very premeditated, orderly fashion—following His laws of blessing and honor.

Rebellion is such a lie and a farce because it simply does not deliver on its promises. It promises freedom but leads to bondage. It promises pleasure but leads to pain. It promises individuality but leads to a loss of identity. It promises a great future and leads to a broken one. It promises control but leads you out of control. It promises a full heart but returns an empty one. Rebellion is a lie.

God always delivers on His promises, and He promises that those who understand and accept His plan for authority will have His supernatural blessing and honor upon their lives! This lesson isn't about putting up with the people who are on your case. It is about finding the process and the path to God's best blessings and getting on it! It is not about simply "obeying your parents"—it is about having a really great life that God blesses every day for the rest of your life. This isn't about a person controlling your life, but rather about God controlling your life.

While the world is questioning authority and reasoning God out of the picture, let's return to His Word and find out His real plan for authority! If you want a really good life, you have to get this!

Authority from God's Perspective

Authority is the right to govern or rule over, or the right to have power or influence over someone or something.

> **Authority** · noun · to have full privilege over. Also, delegated influence, jurisdiction, right to power, strength over.

In this study we will examine many portions of Scripture where God gives us principles of authority in our lives. God has established a structure by which Heaven, Earth, and all living things in them exist in an orderly manner. The more we understand God's structure and submit to it, the more our lives will experience God's purpose and blessing.

As we begin, we must understand that the word *authority* is much bigger than just employers, parents, teachers, police officers, and others who "tell us what to do…." We tend to think of *authority* as it relates to our own little world, but in God's Word, authority is a much broader and more spiritual concept than most people realize.

Let's find out about God's perspective on authority!

1.   Authority Is God's Universal Design

Authority is God's idea! He invented it. He determined that all of creation would have an order—a structure—under which it would function. You might consider authority to be the framework of God's order in creation.

Like a large building has a foundation and a steel frame that provides the structure and the strength for the rest of the building to be established upon, so is authority in our universe and in our lives! Authority is the structure that brings order and stability to every facet of our lives—socially, spiritually and personally.

Consider these thoughts and Scriptures about God's purpose for authority:

All authority and power is ultimately God's.

"God hath spoken once; twice have I heard this; that power belongeth unto God."—PSALM 62:11

"And he changeth the times and the seasons: he removeth kings, and setteth up kings: he giveth wisdom unto the wise, and knowledge to them that know understanding:"—DANIEL 2:21

"And they shall drive thee from men, and thy dwelling shall be with the beasts of the field: they shall make thee to eat grass as oxen, and seven times shall pass over thee, until thou know that the most High ruleth in the kingdom of men, and giveth it to whomsoever he will."—DANIEL 4:32

"…For thine is the kingdom, and the power, and the glory, for ever. Amen."—MATTHEW 6:13B

"But God is the judge: he putteth down one, and setteth up another."—PSALM 75:7

Authority is first seen in God's order of eternity and Heaven.

"Who is gone into heaven, and is on the right hand of God; angels and authorities and powers being made subject unto him."—1 PETER 3:22

God created the universe with structure and order.

"By me kings reign, and princes decree justice. By me princes rule, and nobles, even all the judges of the earth."—PROVERBS 8:15–16

Jesus lived under the authority of His Heavenly Father.

> *"Saying, Father, if thou be willing, remove this cup from me: nevertheless not my will, but thine, be done."*—LUKE 22:42

God designed humanity to function with social structure and authority.

> *"By me kings reign, and princes decree justice. By me princes rule, and nobles, even all the judges of the earth."*—PROVERBS 8:15–16

God designed the home to function with authority structure.

> *"My son, hear the instruction of thy father, and forsake not the law of thy mother:"*
> —PROVERBS 1:8

God designed the church to function with authority structure.

> *"And he gave some, apostles; and some, prophets; and some, evangelists; and some, pastors and teachers; For the perfecting of the saints, for the work of the ministry, for the edifying of the body of Christ:"*—EPHESIANS 4:11–12

2. God Created Four Basic Institutions of Authority

God has established four basic pillars of authority in our lives. We must understand them, accept them, and honor them as the Lord commands. Let's investigate these four basic pillars of authority.

The Word of God is our highest authority.

> *"For the word of God is quick, and powerful, and sharper than any twoedged sword, piercing even to the dividing asunder of soul and spirit, and of the joints and marrow, and is a discerner of the thoughts and intents of the heart."*
> —HEBREWS 4:12

God has given us His Word to be our final authority in all matters of life and faith. A wise Christian will decide to make the Word of God the final authority. Every decision, every choice, every direction in your future should flow from the guiding principles of God's Word.

The home is God's institution of authority.

> *"And, ye fathers, provoke not your children to wrath: but bring them up in the nurture and admonition of the Lord."*—EPHESIANS 6:4

> *"Fathers, provoke not your children to anger, lest they be discouraged."*—COLOSSIANS 3:21

> *"Wives, submit yourselves unto your own husbands, as unto the Lord."*—EPHESIANS 5:22

God established order in the home with the father being the head, the mother supporting that authority, and the children honoring and obeying that authority. God blesses this order and happy homes always understand and experience this kind of structure.

The local church is God's institution of authority.

> *"And I say also unto thee, That thou art Peter,*
> *and upon this rock I will build my church; and*
> *the gates of hell shall not prevail against it."*
> —Matthew 16:18

> *"And if he shall neglect to hear them, tell it unto*
> *the church: but if he neglect to hear the church,*
> *let him be unto thee as an heathen man and a*
> *publican."*—Matthew 18:17

God established the local church as a spiritual authority in our lives. In each church, He calls a pastor to lovingly lead and guide—teaching God's Word and encouraging us to follow Christ. God expects us to commit ourselves to the accountability and structure of a healthy local church. This is His plan. As long as you live, you should have a local church family and a pastor who can help to nurture you by God's grace and encourage you in God's will.

Civil government is God's institution of authority.

> *"Put them in mind to be subject to principalities*
> *and powers, to obey magistrates, to be ready to*
> *every good work,"*—Titus 3:1

> *"Submit yourselves to every ordinance of man*
> *for the Lord's sake: whether it be to the king, as*
> *supreme;"*—1 Peter 2:13

God has established civil government to provide order to our communities, our states, and our nation. These powers are given by God and established by His plan. It is this structure that keeps you safe, protects your freedom, and guarantees you the privilege of building a godly future.

3. Everyone Is Under Authority

No person on the planet is without authority in some form or fashion. God desires for everyone to accept His appointed authority in life. No matter where you go, who you become, or what you choose in life—you will always be subject to God's laws of authority!

Here are a few verses that show how all of creation is under God's structure:

"Let every soul be subject unto the higher powers. For there is no power but of God: the powers that be are ordained of God."—ROMANS 13:1

"Children, obey your parents in the Lord: for this is right."—EPHESIANS 6:1

"Children, obey your parents in all things: for this is well pleasing unto the Lord."
—COLOSSIANS 3:20

"Exhort servants to be obedient unto their own masters, and to please them well in all things; not answering again;"—TITUS 2:9

"Servants, be subject to your masters with all fear; not only to the good and gentle, but also to the froward."—1 PETER 2:18

"Servants, be obedient to them that are your masters according to the flesh, with fear and trembling, in singleness of your heart, as unto Christ;"—EPHESIANS 6:5

"Servants, obey in all things your masters according to the flesh; not with eyeservice, as

menpleasers; but in singleness of heart, fearing God:"—COLOSSIANS 3:22

"Submitting yourselves one to another in the fear of God."—EPHESIANS 5:21

God's principles are clear:

+ Everyone should be under biblical authority.
+ Everyone should be under family authority.
+ Everyone should be under spiritual authority.
+ Everyone is under social and civil authority.

"They say unto him, Caesar's. Then saith he unto them, Render therefore unto Caesar the things which are Caesar's; and unto God the things that are God's."—MATTHEW 22:21

"Put them in mind to be subject to principalities and powers, to obey magistrates, to be ready to every good work,"—TITUS 3:1

4. Earthly Authority Is Not Perfect

It doesn't take long to see that earthly, human authority is never perfect. Humans make mistakes. Parents fail. Those in authority will never be perfect, but God does not expect us to be. In fact, God's command for us to honor and obey authority is not contingent upon whether or not authority is "perfect."

Many people use the failures of authority figures to justify rebellion or disobedience, but God does not grant us this license! He commands us to stand, even when earthly authority fails.

Notice that even Jesus, being perfect, submitted Himself to His imperfect, earthly parents.

"And he went down with them, and came to Nazareth, and was subject unto them: but his mother kept all these sayings in her heart."
—LUKE 2:51

"Submitting yourselves one to another in the fear of God."—EPHESIANS 5:21

Here are a few principles to remember regarding human authorities:

+ The only perfect authority is God and His Word.
+ Earthly authorities will make mistakes.
+ Even Jesus submitted to earthly authority.
+ God commands us to submit to earthly authority as unto Him.
+ God never expects us to disobey or dishonor Him to obey earthly authority.

Two awesome examples of Bible characters who were willingly obedient even to pagan masters are Daniel and Joseph. While they loved and were committed first to God, they understood God's plan for authority, and they accepted the human authority that God had placed in their lives. Look at the verses below:

"But Daniel purposed in his heart that he would not defile himself with the portion of the king's meat, nor with the wine which he drank: therefore he requested of the prince of the eunuchs that he might not defile himself."
—DANIEL 1:8

"Prove thy servants, I beseech thee, ten days; and let them give us pulse to eat, and water to drink."—DANIEL 1:12

"Thou, O king, art a king of kings: for the God of heaven hath given thee a kingdom, power, and strength, and glory."—DANIEL 2:37

"And the LORD *was with Joseph, and he was a prosperous man; and he was in the house of his master the Egyptian."*—GENESIS 39:2

"And Joseph found grace in his sight, and he served him: and he made him overseer over his house, and all that he had he put into his hand."—GENESIS 39:4

"And he left all that he had in Joseph's hand; and he knew not ought he had, save the bread which he did eat. And Joseph was a goodly person, and well favoured."—GENESIS 39:6

5. God's Blessing and Favor Is Promised to Those Under Authority

This is the most wonderful and awesome part of living under God's appointed authority. He promises to bless, honor, and favor those who submit. Those who rebel against God's authority are in for a "train-wreck" of a life! Those who choose to accept God's authority and honor those in authority will receive God's best blessings and favor! What a great promise!

"Honour thy father and thy mother: that thy days may be long upon the land which the LORD *thy God giveth thee."*—EXODUS 20:12

"Honour thy father and thy mother, as the LORD *thy God hath commanded thee; that thy days*

may be prolonged, and that it may go well with thee, in the land which the LORD thy God giveth thee."—DEUTERONOMY 5:16

"Honour thy father and mother; (which is the first commandment with promise;)" —EPHESIANS 6:2

"And the child Samuel grew on, and was in favour both with the LORD, and also with men."—1 SAMUEL 2:26

"For thou, LORD, wilt bless the righteous; with favour wilt thou compass him as with a shield."—PSALM 5:12

"So shalt thou find favour and good understanding in the sight of God and man."—PROVERBS 3:4

"He that diligently seeketh good procureth favour: but he that seeketh mischief, it shall come unto him."—PROVERBS 11:27

"A good man obtaineth favour of the LORD: but a man of wicked devices will he condemn." —PROVERBS 12:2

"Good understanding giveth favour: but the way of transgressors is hard."—PROVERBS 13:15

To summarize, here are the key principles:

+ Choosing to honor authority is a choice to honor God.
+ God's blessings only come through God's order.
+ God promises blessing and favor to those who honor authority.

6. Authority Is Given for Our Protection, Safety, and Edification

Authority is actually a blessing! Without authority we are easy prey for Satan. Authority stands in the gap and provides a spiritual hedge or wall of protection around us to prevent Satan and his traps from ruining our lives.

Many people believe that authority is bent on controlling or robbing fun. Nothing could be further from the truth! Godly authorities serve as your spiritual protection in the battle for your future.

When you accept authority, it's like accepting a wonderful wall of safety around your life. From within that wall, God desires to bless you, build you, and prepare you for an awesome future!

When you resist authority, you are only resisting your own safety and blessing! Think about it. Don't hurt yourself by fighting authority!

> *"Let every soul be subject unto the higher powers. For there is no power but of God: the powers that be are ordained of God. Whosoever therefore resisteth the power, resisteth the ordinance of God: and they that resist shall receive to themselves damnation. For rulers are not a terror to good works, but to the evil. Wilt thou then not be afraid of the power? do that which is good, and thou shalt have praise of the same: For he is the minister of God to thee for good. But if thou do that which is evil, be afraid; for he beareth not the sword in vain: for he is the minister of God, a revenger to execute wrath upon him that doeth evil."*—ROMANS 13:1–4

"Not for that we have dominion over your faith, but are helpers of your joy: for by faith ye stand."—2 CORINTHIANS 1:24

"For though I should boast somewhat more of our authority, which the Lord hath given us for edification, and not for your destruction, I should not be ashamed:"—2 CORINTHIANS 10:8

"And he gave some, apostles; and some, prophets; and some, evangelists; and some, pastors and teachers; For the perfecting of the saints, for the work of the ministry, for the edifying of the body of Christ: Till we all come in the unity of the faith, and of the knowledge of the Son of God, unto a perfect man, unto the measure of the stature of the fulness of Christ: That we henceforth be no more children, tossed to and fro, and carried about with every wind of doctrine, by the sleight of men, and cunning craftiness, whereby they lie in wait to deceive; But speaking the truth in love, may grow up into him in all things, which is the head, even Christ:"—EPHESIANS 4:11–15

Here are the principles we learn in these passages:

- God desires first to protect us spiritually.
- God desires secondly to protect us physically.
- God desires to edify and grow us.
- God's first line of help in your spiritual battles is your authorities.

7. Everyone Eventually Becomes Someone's Authority

This is a scary thought! Eventually, you will be someone's authority in life. This is inevitable! You cannot avoid it. In fact, right now you are preparing for your future position of authority. You are sowing seeds that you will one day reap. Learning how to honor and respect authority now is the best preparation for being a godly authority figure later!

> *"Remember now thy Creator in the days of thy youth, while the evil days come not, nor the years draw nigh, when thou shalt say, I have no pleasure in them;"*—ECCLESIASTES 12:1

> *"Let no man despise thy youth; but be thou an example of the believers, in word, in conversation, in charity, in spirit, in faith, in purity."*—1 TIMOTHY 4:12

Think about this:

- Everyone eventually fulfills a position of authority in someone else's life.
- Your future position of authority is a position of service.
- Your future position of authority is a position of spiritual protection.
- Your submission to authority now is training for your future as authority.

8. Authority Should Be Honored and Submitted to as unto the Lord

"Wherefore ye must needs be subject, not only for wrath, but also for conscience sake. For for this cause pay ye tribute also: for they are God's ministers, attending continually upon this very thing. Render therefore to all their dues: tribute to whom tribute is due; custom to whom custom; fear to whom fear; honour to whom honour."—ROMANS 13:5–7

"And they answered Joshua, saying, All that thou commandest us we will do, and whithersoever thou sendest us, we will go. According as we hearkened unto Moses in all things, so will we hearken unto thee: only the LORD thy God be with thee, as he was with Moses. Whosoever he be that doth rebel against thy commandment, and will not hearken unto thy words in all that thou commandest him, he shall be put to death: only be strong and of a good courage."
—JOSHUA 1:16–18

"Put them in mind to be subject to principalities and powers, to obey magistrates, to be ready to every good work,"—TITUS 3:1

"Submit yourselves to every ordinance of man for the Lord's sake: whether it be to the king, as supreme; Or unto governors, as unto them that are sent by him for the punishment of evildoers, and for the praise of them that do well. For so is the will of God, that with well doing ye may put to silence the ignorance of foolish men:

As free, and not using your liberty for a cloke
of maliciousness, but as the servants of God.
Honour all men. Love the brotherhood. Fear
God. Honour the king."—1 PETER 2:13–17

God makes it clear that He commands us to honor and submit to authority. To *honor* means "to value or to make weighty." Honoring and obeying are two vastly different things.

If you are a young person, you can obey without honoring, but you cannot honor without obeying!

For all young people, the choices are basic.

Three basic responses of young people to authority:

+ Outward obedience with inward dishonor
+ Outward obedience with inward honor
+ Outward defiance with inward rebellion

9. Authority Should Be Appreciated, Encouraged, and Supported in Prayer

Most people don't think of this point at all! Those who serve you as authority figures are merely human—they are people who could use your love, your encouragement, and your prayer. Rather than resent them, avoid them, gossip about them, and disdain them—consider a different approach. Consider doing what God says. Consider being their friend, their supporter, their encourager! Your authorities could become your best friends if you would see them and their love in a new way.

The Bible is clear that God is greatly displeased with those who willfully and openly speak against and despise authorities:

"But chiefly them that walk after the flesh in the lust of uncleanness, and despise government. Presumptuous are they, selfwilled, they are not afraid to speak evil of dignities. Whereas angels, which are greater in power and might, bring not railing accusation against them before the Lord."—2 Peter 2:10–11

"Likewise also these filthy dreamers defile the flesh, despise dominion, and speak evil of dignities."—Jude 8

Rather than resist and despise, choose to encourage, support, pray for, and uplift those who fight a vicious spiritual battle on your behalf! Some authority figure in your life right now needs your encouragement! Go give it to them.

There are four things you can do to honor your authorities:

- Obey willingly those who serve as your authorities.
- Appreciate those who serve as your authorities.
- Encourage those who serve as your authorities.
- Pray for those who serve as your authorities.

10. Someday Everyone Will Bow before Christ's Authority

When all is said and done, you will bow before the authority of Jesus Christ. He will rule and reign whether you accept His authority or not. Look at what God says:

"And he hath on his vesture and on his thigh a name written, KING OF KINGS, AND LORD OF LORDS."—Revelation 19:16

"Which he wrought in Christ, when he raised him from the dead, and set him at his own right hand in the heavenly places, Far above all principality, and power, and might, and dominion, and every name that is named, not only in this world, but also in that which is to come:"—EPHESIANS 1:20–21

"For it is written, As I live, saith the Lord, every knee shall bow to me, and every tongue shall confess to God."—ROMANS 14:11

"That at the name of Jesus every knee should bow, of things in heaven, and things in earth, and things under the earth;"—PHILIPPIANS 2:10

"And he is the head of the body, the church: who is the beginning, the firstborn from the dead; that in all things he might have the preeminence."—COLOSSIANS 1:18

Honoring and obeying authority now is merely preparation for the day when we will all be directly under the power and presence of Jesus Christ! Honor Him today by honoring those He has set up in your life!

Conclusion

Your best life will be found within the bounds of authority!

God's best blessings are reserved for those who truly understand, accept, and honor His authority and the authority figures that He places in our lives.

How have you been treating authority in your life? Let God have His way and choose to live a life of honor!

Questions for Personal Study
Biblical Authority

1. What principles most spoke to your heart in this lesson?

2. List the names of the godly authority figures in your life right now.

3. In what ways are you honoring authority and in what ways are you dishonoring authority?

4. Describe how dishonoring authority has hurt you in the past.

5. Write out and memorize Romans 13:1 about higher powers.

Life Relationships

Pleasing God in My Relationships with Others

*"Be kindly affectioned one to another with brotherly love; in honour preferring one another; Not slothful in business; fervent in spirit; serving the Lord; Rejoicing in hope; patient in tribulation; continuing instant in prayer; Distributing to the necessity of saints; given to hospitality. Bless them which persecute you: bless, and curse not. Rejoice with them that do rejoice, and weep with them that weep. Be of the same mind one toward another. Mind not high things, but condescend to men of low estate. Be not wise in your own conceits. Recompense to no man evil for evil. Provide things honest in the sight of all men. If it be possible, as much as lieth in you, live peaceably with all men. Dearly beloved, avenge not yourselves, but rather give place unto wrath: for it is written, Vengeance is mine; I will repay, saith the Lord. Therefore if thine enemy hunger, feed him; if he thirst, give him drink: for in so doing thou shalt heap coals of fire on his head. Be not overcome of evil, but overcome evil with good."—*ROMANS 12:10–21

"Let all bitterness, and wrath, and anger, and clamour, and evil speaking, be put away from you, with all malice: And be ye kind one to another, tenderhearted, forgiving one another, even as God for Christ's sake hath forgiven you."—EPHESIANS 4:31–32

People, People, People...

Has it ever occurred to you that people come from people? Of course, God gives us life. Yet, from your very first moment of life, you were *from* people, *in* another person, and *surrounded* by people. Since the moment of your birth you have been handled by people, cared for by people, and interrelated to people every day of your life. I sure hope you like people—if not, you're kind of stuck!

In fact, if you are a young person, right now you are dependent upon people. Your life, your dwelling, your clothing, your food, your health, and your daily emotional stability greatly depend upon the people that God has placed in your life. They taught you to walk, to talk, to eat, to potty, and even to stay away from electrical outlets!

To this day people are teaching you academic subjects, sports, music, Bible, and life. You are depending upon their sacrifice to keep you sustained. You are dependent upon their love to give you stability. You are dependent upon their faithfulness to help you prepare for your future. You are dependent upon their knowledge to keep you safe and secure.

Now and for the rest of your life, God intends to connect you with others—people who love you and whom you should love in return. And in the soon coming future, the tables will turn. Most likely, you will soon find some other person depending upon you for something. This will happen first when you get a job. Then it will take a major leap forward when you get married. And then when kids come along—it's all over.

Sooner than later, someone else is going to be depending completely upon you—for life, for food, for clothes, for shelter, for safety, for provision. Sooner or later, you will wake up every day knowing that people are counting on you, trusting you, relying upon you to do the right thing.

You see, life is about relationships! Life revolves around our connectedness to other people that God has placed in our lives. And more than most other life details, He cares about how we care for these relationships.

Life is about relationships, and as a teenager, you are in major preparation mode for future relationships. You are getting ready to be a spouse, a parent, an employee, etc. God has designed life to have early relationships that prepare you for adult relationships. Every relationship in your life now is preparing you for someone special in the future.

Here is an interesting set of questions to ponder: What kind of spouse do you want your husband or wife to have? What kind of parent do your kids deserve? What kind of employee do you want to be? What kind of church member will your future pastor and church family deserve? What kind of grandparent do you want to be?

Scary? Sure! But sooner than you think, you will be fulfilling these roles in vital relationships that God brings into your life. Whether you want to or not, you are preparing now. You are becoming the person that you will be in these relationships. This study is all about making the most of today's relationships and preparing for tomorrow's at the same time!

One more thought. Has it occurred to you that you won't always have the relationships you have today? You won't always have your parents or your siblings. You won't always have those grandparents or your pastor. You won't always be where you are with the people you know right now. Life will change. Time will pass. The relationships you know today will at some point conclude. What if that happened today? Would you regret not having healthier relationships? Would you wish you had done something differently?

Let's discover God's plan for investing our best into every relationship of life!

God Connects People for a Purpose

God created people, and God connects people! He designed our lives not to be independent, but dependent and interdependent—first upon Him, then upon each other. You were created to have relationships in your life that are vital to your development as a person and as a child of God.

Now and throughout your life, God cares much more about your relationships than your accomplishments! He cares about who you are with Him and with others!

Your accomplishments and achievements in life do not matter if you are sacrificing your relationships along the way! People are more important to God than anything we could do with our lives. Your life matters most as you love and live for people—serving, giving, and investing.

In all of our lives there are vital, high-priority relationships, and there are lesser priority, secondary relationships. That is not to say that some people are less important than others, but to say that some relationships are God-given essentials in your life, and others are not as essential. For instance, your relationship with your parents is far more vital than your relationship with your coach or a friend from school.

As you grow, Satan will always try to replace vital relationships in your life with non-vital relationships or with lesser things! For instance, he would rather you be close to your friends (non-vital) than to your family (vital)! He would rather you retreat to your room with your headphones than actually interact and develop a relationship with those in your family. He would rather you love your job more than your kids!

More than ever in our culture, Satan is killing vital relationships and causing us to spend time with empty things like careers, video games, TV, etc.

More than you realize at this age, your life is about healthy vital relationships! The more you focus on nurturing those vital relationships, the more your life will be joyful, full, and blessed.

Let's discover God's plan for the relationships of life.

1. God Has Designed All of the Relationships in My Life

> *"And whatsoever ye do, do it heartily, as to the Lord, and not unto men; Knowing that of the Lord ye shall receive the reward of the inheritance: for ye serve the Lord Christ."*—COLOSSIANS 3:23–24

This verse was written as a conclusion to a passage dealing with many of our life relationships and God's instructions regarding them! God is saying that in every relationship we are to conduct ourselves "heartily, as to the Lord"!

Every earthly relationship is more about our heart for God than our heart toward men!

Every earthly relationship is placed in my life by God for a purpose!

First, let's consider the vital relationships and the secondary relationships that God places in our lives, both now and in the future!

The vital relationships that God designed our lives to include:

+ Relationship with God
+ Relationships with Parents/Family (or primary authority)
+ Relationships with Siblings
+ Relationship with Pastor and Church Family
+ Relationships with Elders/Teachers

Secondary relationships that God may allow you to enjoy:

+ Relationships with Extended Family
+ Relationships with Friends
+ Relationships with Coworkers/Teammates

If you are a young person, the vital relationships that will be a part of your future include:

+ Relationship with God
+ Relationship with Spouse
+ Relationships with Children
+ Relationship with Pastor and Church Family

Secondary relationships that God may allow you to enjoy:

+ Relationship with Employer
+ Relationships with Extended Family
+ Relationships with Friends
+ Relationships with Coworkers/Associates

2. God Commands Me to Prefer Others with Brotherly Love

"Be kindly affectioned one to another with brotherly love; in honour preferring one another;" —ROMANS 12:10

"And above all these things put on charity, which is the bond of perfectness. And let the peace of God rule in your hearts, to the which also ye are called in one body; and be ye thankful." —COLOSSIANS 3:14–15

"Beloved, let us love one another: for love is of God; and every one that loveth is born of God, and knoweth God."—1 JOHN 4:7

"Beloved, if God so loved us, we ought also to love one another."—1 JOHN 4:11

"Seeing ye have purified your souls in obeying the truth through the Spirit unto unfeigned love of the brethren, see that ye love one another with a pure heart fervently:"—1 PETER 1:22

"A new commandment I give unto you, That ye love one another; as I have loved you, that ye also love one another."—JOHN 13:34

This command applies to all of my life relationships. This is a basic love and respect that is due to every person as the unique creation of God.

People are often, out of immaturity, inconsiderate and hurtful in relationships towards others—especially family members. As you grow spiritually it is vital that you allow God to remove this childish spirit of hurtfulness and replace it with a godly spirit of brotherly love towards others.

This command should move you to action. You should be the initiator of loving actions and expressions in all of your relationships!

Often we are self-centered and expect others to act upon us—to show love to us first. This causes us to be relationally passive, waiting for others to express love or communicate to us first. Then when someone doesn't fulfill our expectations, we withdraw or resent the fact. In almost every case, if we think about it, it is within our power to make the first move—to express love first.

It is the will of God that we would act first—express love in all of our relationships on our own without waiting for someone else to initiate or even to respond. This is what selfless brotherly love is all about.

You are demonstrating a great heart of maturity when you can initiate love and communication in your relationships—rather than waiting for someone else to!

To put it simply—don't wait for others to talk to you or express love to you. Choose to go to them and express love first!

3. My Relationship with God Should Be My Life's First Priority

"I will praise thee, O Lord my God, with all my heart: and I will glorify thy name for evermore."
—PSALM 86:12

"Let us hear the conclusion of the whole matter: Fear God, and keep his commandments: for this is the whole duty of man."—ECCLESIASTES 12:13

"Jesus said unto him, Thou shalt love the Lord thy God with all thy heart, and with all thy soul, and with all thy mind."—MATTHEW 22:37

"And thou shalt love the Lord thy God with all thy heart, and with all thy soul, and with all thy mind, and with all thy strength: this is the first commandment."—MARK 12:30

"If any man come to me, and hate not his father, and mother, and wife, and children, and brethren, and sisters, yea, and his own life also, he cannot be my disciple."—LUKE 14:26

"Little children, keep yourselves from idols. Amen."—1 JOHN 5:21

"Whether therefore ye eat, or drink, or whatsoever ye do, do all to the glory of God."
—1 CORINTHIANS 10:31

Without question, God desires and deserves the first priority and place in your life! He created you, He saved you, He owns you, and He belongs on the throne of your heart.

God is a personal God. Over and over in Scripture He invites you into His presence to know Him, to relate to Him personally. He doesn't want to be a far-off figure in your life, but a very present friend—a close intimate relationship of the heart!

When you are drawing close to God and giving Him first place in your life, every other relationship of your life will take on a new perspective. When God is not in His place, life becomes confusing, frustrating, and overwhelming. But when He is first, He takes care of all of your needs, questions, and problems.

Look at God's promises concerning our personal relationships with Him:

"Even the youths shall faint and be weary, and the young men shall utterly fall: But they that wait upon the LORD shall renew their strength; they

shall mount up with wings as eagles; they shall run, and not be weary; and they shall walk, and not faint."—ISAIAH 40:30–31

"The LORD is nigh unto them that are of a broken heart; and saveth such as be of a contrite spirit" —PSALM 34:18

"I love them that love me; and those that seek me early shall find me."—PROVERBS 8:17

"Behold, I stand at the door, and knock: if any man hear my voice, and open the door, I will come in to him, and will sup with him, and he with me." —REVELATION 3:20

"Call unto me, and I will answer thee, and show thee great and mighty things, which thou knowest not."—JEREMIAH 33:3

"Draw nigh to God, and he will draw nigh to you…" —JAMES 4:8

"Glory and honour are in his presence; strength and gladness are in his place."—1 CHRONICLES 16:27

"Thou wilt keep him in perfect peace, whose mind is stayed on thee: because he trusteth in thee. Trust ye in the LORD for ever: for in the LORD JEHOVAH is everlasting strength:"—ISAIAH 26:3–4

4. My Relationship with My Parents Prepares Me for My Future Spouse

"Honour thy father and thy mother, as the LORD thy God hath commanded thee; that thy

days may be prolonged, and that it may go well with thee, in the land which the LORD thy God giveth thee."—DEUTERONOMY 5:16

"Honour thy father and mother; (which is the first commandment with promise;)" —EPHESIANS 6:2

"Likewise, ye wives, be in subjection to your own husbands;"—1 PETER 3:1

"Likewise, ye husbands, dwell with them according to knowledge, giving honour unto the wife, as unto the weaker vessel, and as being heirs together of the grace of life; that your prayers be not hindered."—1 PETER 3:7

First, we must recognize that for a teenager, this relationship should be second only to God! No one is as important to your life, your happiness, and your spiritual growth as your parents! You must make your relationship with them the priority of your life after God.

Also, it is vital that you see this relationship as a training time for your future marriage! One day you will need to love, honor, and submit to your own spouse. Growing up under your parent's love and learning to love them selflessly is the best preparation for a happy marriage.

Young man, you will one day treat your wife the way you treat your mother! Young lady, you will one day treat your husband the way you treat your father!

Learn to love your parents now and to have a close friendship with them so that you can one day transfer those relational and biblical principles into your marriage!

5. My Relationships with My Siblings Prepare Me for My Future Children

"And, ye fathers, provoke not your children to wrath: but bring them up in the nurture and admonition of the Lord."—EPHESIANS 6:4

It is no secret that brothers and sisters are masterful at provoking each other to anger. Sibling rivalry is a carnal thing—it happens because we let the flesh rule our lives rather than the spirit.

God doesn't intend for your relationship with your siblings to be one of fighting, anger, and jealousy. Growing up with siblings is your opportunity to learn to honor and nurture those to whom you are the closest.

The saying "familiarity breeds contempt" does not have to be true! Because you are familiar with your siblings' flaws does not mean you must resent them or resist them. You can choose to love, to honor, to prefer one another as Christ did.

One of the best training grounds for learning to nurture and love your future children is right in your own home while you are growing up. If you can nurture your brother or sister, you will one day be an excellent parent! Your kids deserve that.

6. My Relationships with My Teachers/Elders Prepare Me for My Future Employer

"Let every soul be subject unto the higher powers. For there is no power but of God: the powers that be are ordained of God."—ROMANS 13:1

Learning to live under authority while you are young is preparation for living under authority when you become an adult. You will one day have a career or a vocation—and with it, authorities to whom you will answer.

Learning to honor and respect teachers and elders now is God's way of giving you a training ground for your future!

7. My Relationship with My Pastor and Church Family Is Vital to All My Life

"And I will give you pastors according to mine heart, which shall feed you with knowledge and understanding."—JEREMIAH 3:15

"And he gave some, apostles; and some, prophets; and some, evangelists; and some, pastors and teachers; For the perfecting of the saints, for the work of the ministry, for the edifying of the body of Christ:"—EPHESIANS 4:11–12

"Only let your conversation be as it becometh the gospel of Christ: that whether I come and see you, or else be absent, I may hear of your affairs, that ye stand fast in one spirit, with one mind striving together for the faith of the gospel;"—PHILIPPIANS 1:27

Jesus loved the church so much that He gave His life for it! And in every church He places leaders—pastors who are commanded to love, nurture, and lead the church family to honor the Lord.

Then He commands us to assemble for the purposes of worship, preaching, growth, fellowship, and service. The church is God's idea, and while no church or pastor is perfect, having a good relationship with your pastor and church family is essential to your spiritual growth and health!

No matter where your life takes you, always establish a healthy relationship with your pastor and your church family! God will bless you greatly through this priority!

8. As a Christian, Every Life Relationship Is an Opportunity for Ministry

"For the Son of man is come to seek and to save that which was lost."—LUKE 19:10

"But we were gentle among you, even as a nurse cherisheth her children: So being affectionately desirous of you, we were willing to have imparted unto you, not the gospel of God only, but also our own souls, because ye were dear unto us. For ye remember, brethren, our labour and travail: for labouring night and day, because we would not be chargeable unto any of you, we preached unto you the gospel of God. Ye are witnesses, and God also, how holily and justly and unblameably we behaved ourselves among you that believe: As ye know how we exhorted and comforted and charged every one of you, as a father doth his children, That ye would walk worthy of God, who hath called you unto his kingdom and glory."—1 THESSALONIANS 2:7–12

No relationship of your life is an accident! God authors and ordains every single interaction you have with another human being, and He desires for you to view each interaction as a chance to minister Christ's love to others!

No matter where you are, people have needs and God desires for you to help to meet those needs by His grace.

Your whole life will be filled with Divine appointments—moments when your life intersects with someone else's for a reason. The more you understand God's touch behind these moments, the more you can begin allowing His Holy Spirit to fill and guide you into "how" you must minister to each unique person.

Every relationship is an opportunity to witness for Christ or to share His love with others!

It is time you realize that you can minister to everyone—parents, pastor, siblings, friends, etc.! Start viewing every relationship in your life as a chance to serve!

9. God's Desire Is That I Would Immediately Resolve Problems in My Relationships

"Moreover if thy brother shall trespass against thee, go and tell him his fault between thee and him alone: if he shall hear thee, thou hast gained thy brother."—MATTHEW 18:15

"Therefore if thou bring thy gift to the altar, and there rememberest that thy brother hath ought against thee; Leave there thy gift before the altar, and go thy way; first be reconciled to thy brother, and then come and offer thy gift."—MATTHEW 5:23–24

"But now ye also put off all these; anger, wrath, malice, blasphemy, filthy communication out of your mouth. Lie not one to another, seeing that ye have put off the old man with his deeds; And have put on the new man, which is renewed in knowledge after the image of him

that created him: Where there is neither Greek nor Jew, circumcision nor uncircumcision, Barbarian, Scythian, bond nor free: but Christ is all, and in all. Put on therefore, as the elect of God, holy and beloved, bowels of mercies, kindness, humbleness of mind, meekness, longsuffering; Forbearing one another, and forgiving one another, if any man have a quarrel against any: even as Christ forgave you, so also do ye. And above all these things put on charity, which is the bond of perfectness. And let the peace of God rule in your hearts, to the which also ye are called in one body; and be ye thankful."—COLOSSIANS 3:8–15

"Let all bitterness, and wrath, and anger, and clamour, and evil speaking, be put away from you, with all malice: And be ye kind one to another, tenderhearted, forgiving one another, even as God for Christ's sake hath forgiven you."—EPHESIANS 4:31–32

"With all lowliness and meekness, with longsuffering, forbearing one another in love;"
—EPHESIANS 4:2

The word *forbear* means "to endure" or literally "to put up with."

God never gives us permission to let arguments or offenses go unresolved! There will always be problems in relationships, but God expects us to go to that relationship and to settle that problem with a spirit of selfless love and forgiveness.

I cannot control the actions of others, but I can control or choose my treatment of others and my response to their actions. I can do everything within my power to "live peaceably with all men."

Do you have unresolved arguments with family or friends? Do you have open issues or wounds with others? Have you hurt or offended others in your life? God's command to you is that you would go to that person immediately and make your relationship right.

10. God Teaches Me How to Treat Various Kinds of People

In our text at the chapter's beginning and in other verses, we see admonitions for treating all kinds of people. Here are just a few as we conclude:

- Those who are my enemies—love them
- Those who hurt or are suffering—weep with them
- Those who scorn or cause division—avoid them (Romans 16)
- Those who have hurt me—forgive them
- Those who are poor or "of low estate"—condescend to them (lower yourself with them)
- Those who are another race or nationality—"be of the same mind one toward another"
- Those who are lost without Christ—overcome evil with good, witness to them
- Those who are in need—give to them
- Those who are lonely—be hospitable towards them

The common denominator that should rule all of our relationships is the love of Christ! By God's grace I can and should love everybody that I come into contact with.

Conclusion

- Every relationship in your life now is preparing you for other relationships!
- Every relationship holds a divine purpose and an opportunity for ministry!
- Every relationship matters more to God than your life's accomplishments.
- Choose that you will value people the way that God values them!
- Choose that you will love others the way God commands!
- Choose that you will make vital relationships your highest priorities in life!
- Choose to build healthy, right relationships as unto the Lord.

"If it be possible, as much as lieth in you, live peaceably with all men."—ROMANS 12:18

Questions for Personal Study
Life Relationships

1. Describe the difference between a vital relationship and a secondary relationship.

2. List the vital relationships that God has placed in your life right now.

3. List the secondary relationships that God has placed in your life right now.

4. Write out one thing you can do that would make each of your vital relationships stronger.

5. How do you tend to deal with conflict in your relationships? Is there something you need to deal with now?

6. Pray and ask the Lord to help you maintain healthy relationships that honor Him.

CHAPTER NINE

Biblical Principles for Dating

Preparing My Heart for a Lifetime of Love

"Keep thy heart with all diligence; for out of it are the issues of life."—PROVERBS 4:23

The Purity Risk

If I told you that you could have one dollar right now or ten million dollars eight years from now, which would you choose? It seems like a pretty easy decision. If you have half a brain, you would opt for the ten million and choose to wait a few years. I think you would ultimately say that the ten million was well worth the wait!

Let me ask you another question. If you had a two-carat diamond worth thousands of dollars, and you needed someone to take care of it for you, to whom would you give it? Would you hand it to any stranger off the street? How about to a five-year-old child? Probably not. You wouldn't trust the stranger, and the child wouldn't be ready to handle such a weighty responsibility. Instead, you would hand that valuable jewel to someone you truly trusted to guard and protect it.

If you can understand these two illustrations, then you can understand the risks of dating too seriously, too soon and you can understand the importance of trusting your parents and spiritual leaders to help you protect your purity until you get married.

Satan and the world's culture will often come to you with a very attractive offer—one dollar's worth of pleasure right now! His goal is to rob you of the ten million. His goal is to sabotage your future by trapping you while you are young and naïve. It is amazing how many Christians are taking the bait. They are trading a lifetime of godly love for a quick moment of pleasure that they will soon deeply regret.

In contrast, God has a fantastic plan to provide you with "a billion dollars' worth" of fulfillment and true life-time love, but He asks that you wait for the right person at the right time. If you can see past the end of your nose, you will opt for God's plan. You will wait and trust Him, and one day you will be so very glad that you waited!

Like the diamond in that illustration, God has given you something very precious—a pure life and a future. He intends to intersect your life at the right time with the right person according to His perfect will. At that time, you will fall madly in love with the person of your dreams and begin to build a life and family together by God's wonderful design. Now is not the time to fulfill these desires. Now is not the time to hand that valuable treasure to a stranger, but rather the time to grow and prepare for God's best.

Satan wants you to hand your valuable purity to a stranger. He wants you to carelessly throw your future away completely unaware of its value and significance. God's instructions to you are to guard your heart—to protect your purity and keep it safe until the day He unites you with the right person at the right time.

Will you choose one dollar's worth of pleasure now, or will you guard your heart and wait for God's grand reward? Will you hand your purity to the wrong person or will you trust those who love you deeply to protect it and guide you into God's promise for your future? These are the important questions you will answer as you decide your course on the dating issue.

While so many people in the world are dating for all the wrong reasons and in the wrong way, this study will help you understand God's true plan and encourage you to trust God and wait on His timing. These principles will show you what is really at stake and what you are risking if you become involved too seriously too soon in a dating relationship.

So, I ask you, do you want one dollar's worth of pleasure now or ten million dollar's worth of pleasure later? God does not want to keep you from true love; He just wants it to be true—the right person at the right time. He wants you to live your life with no regrets, and He wants your marriage to be the very best that it can be!

The real question is, do you trust God or yourself? Let's discover God's plan for these new feelings that we call "attraction" to the opposite sex.

The Truth about Dating

The Bible give us a wealth of principles for growing and preparing our lives for marriage and family. It does give principles for healthy relationships that honor the Lord.

The world's definition of dating revolves around emotional attraction that starts too young and inflates quickly! God does not intend for you to give your heart away to many different people over a long period of time. He does not intend for you to idolize someone or some relationship. He does not intend for your youthful lusts to become enlarged because of culture's pressure.

If Satan has his way, he will enlarge your desires, pervert them, and draw you away from God after some boyfriend or girlfriend. He wants you to be consumed with being "liked" to the point that you become controlled by emotions and peer pressure.

This study is all about avoiding that slippery slope of emotional attraction. It is about looking further down the road and understanding guiding principles about friendships, relationships, and preparing for a future marriage.

The most important consideration is that you are now preparing for your future spouse! You must do so God's way. Let's take a look at the principles that will protect us and guide us to a happy future in love.

1. We Must Understand God-given Desires and Satan's Perversion of Them

"For all that is in the world, the lust of the flesh, and the lust of the eyes, and the pride of life, is not of the Father, but is of the world."—1 John 2:16

"How that they told you there should be mockers in the last time, who should walk after their own ungodly lusts."—Jude 18

Attraction between men and ladies is a wonderful, God-given part of life! There is nothing "wrong" with these attractions. They are God's gift to us for His glory!

But, the devil desires to pervert and enlarge those attractions. He desires to reduce them to nothing more than fleshly lusts—impure, physical desires. Then he desires to draw you astray with those physical desires into an impure lifestyle.

The world and secular entertainment lie about love and sex, but God always tells the truth!

God does not want us living for our fleshly desires. He says that they "war against the soul." He says that they are ungodly and that we should not "walk after them" like the world does.

2. We Must Restrain Our Desires until God's Time and Plan

"Teaching us that, denying ungodliness and worldly lusts, we should live soberly, righteously, and godly, in this present world;"—Titus 2:12

"Dearly beloved, I beseech you as strangers and pilgrims, abstain from fleshly lusts, which war against the soul;"—1 Peter 2:11

"But every man is tempted, when he is drawn away of his own lust, and enticed. Then when lust hath conceived, it bringeth forth sin: and sin, when it is finished, bringeth forth death."—James 1:14–15

"Now concerning the things whereof ye wrote unto me: It is good for a man not to touch a woman."—1 Corinthians 7:1

"I made a covenant with mine eyes; why then should I think upon a maid?"—Job 31:1

> *"For this is the will of God, even your sanctification, that ye should abstain from fornication:"*
> —1 THESSALONIANS 4:3

Fulfilled prematurely and inappropriately, our physical desires become fleshly lusts that war against us and destroy us! Walking after these lusts takes our lives down a destructive path that God warns us to avoid.

Yet, fulfilled in God's time with God's will in a spouse, these desires become blessings to our marriage and family.

God's will now is that you understand the truth, trust the truth, and restrain your physical desires until He ordains the right person and the right time.

Our young adult lives are the time when we truly learn to be faithful in marriage by first being faithful to God. If you can discover how to restrain your physical desires by God's power now, then you will have the character qualities to remain faithful to your spouse for the rest of your life!

3. The Primary Purpose of Dating Is to Prepare for and Discover My Future Spouse

> *"Let no man despise thy youth; but be thou an example of the believers, in word, in conversation, in charity, in spirit, in faith, in purity."*—1 TIMOTHY 4:12

The world's purpose in dating is to fulfill emotional desires and heart-needs that only God and your parents can truly fill when you are young. Don't fall into this trap! Don't get caught up in an emotional attraction that leads your heart away from the Lord and your family.

In actuality, youth is a growing time—a preparation time. It is not a time to pretend to be married or to pretend to belong to someone. It is a time to prepare for when you will truly belong to someone for life!

God says in the verse above that our lives should grow in purity, in faith, in spirit, in charity, in word, and in conversation (lifestyle). He says that our young lives should be shining examples of His goodness and grace.

Decide now that you will prepare for your future spouse by being godly while you are young!

4. Exclusive Youthful Dating Relationships Present Enormous Emotional, Physical, and Spiritual Risks

Dating always presents risks for everyone, but dating too seriously at too young an age increases those risks greatly!

Emotional Risks

> "Keep thy heart with all diligence; for out of it are the issues of life."—PROVERBS 4:23

> "Then this Daniel was preferred above the presidents and princes, because an excellent spirit was in him; and the king thought to set him over the whole realm."—DANIEL 6:3

Satan wants your spirit! He wants your attitude. He wants to get your young heart ensnared in relationships that take you away. He wants your heart to drift from God, parents, and godly friends. This is a dangerous process.

Remember this—your heart belongs to God and to your parents. Do not give it away to anyone else until the Lord makes it clear that it's the right person at the right time! The following is a short list of the emotional risks:

- Emotional attraction only—clinging to a person rather than to God
- Emotional attachment—giving a person the devotion that God deserves
- Emotional deception—being led away by our lusts
- Emotional pain at break-up—being devastated when the relationship ends

Physical Risks

> "Dearly beloved, I beseech you as strangers and pilgrims, abstain from fleshly lusts, which war against the soul;"—1 PETER 2:11

Satan wants your physical purity! He wants to keep you from ever experiencing a physical relationship in marriage that is healthy, holy, and happy for a lifetime! As Isaac and Rebekah in Genesis 24, commit to living godly and pure before the Lord. If you give away your purity while you are young, this decision will "war against your soul" for the rest of your life!

The following is a short list of the physical risks:

- Becoming physical in a relationship that isn't ready to be such
- Physical desires growing and creating greater temptations
- Physical desires reaching a point where they cannot be reversed
- Physical desires leading to losing our purity and hurting our lives

Spiritual Risks

"Wherefore, my dearly beloved, flee from idolatry."—1 CORINTHIANS 10:14

For many young people, dating becomes idolatry. This other person becomes someone who takes the place of God in their lives. Their devotion, their time, their communication and their worship go to this person rather than to God.

Don't allow a friendship to take the place of God in your life. It's a trap! Take a look at the spiritual risks:

+ Neglecting my relationship with God
+ Replacing God with another person
+ Not growing spiritually because of a relationship
+ Being led astray from God's will because of a friend's will

5. God Uses Authority to Confirm a Right or to Protect from a Wrong Relationship

"Honour thy father and thy mother, as the LORD thy God hath commanded thee; that thy days may be prolonged, and that it may go well with thee, in the land which the LORD thy God giveth thee."—DEUTERONOMY 5:16

In Genesis 24, Isaac and Rebekah are brought together, fall in love, and get married. The story recounts the amazing will of God in bringing them together and how He confirmed His will.

One of the primary ways that Isaac and Rebekah knew that they were right for each other was because godly parents and authorities in their lives affirmed God's hand in the situation. They had never met each other, but they were right for each other. One way they knew they were right for each other was that they sided with godly authority!

- ◆ Don't even begin dating someone, ever, without your parents' approval of that person.
- ◆ Young men—get a father's permission before you pursue or win the heart of a girl.
- ◆ Young ladies—trust your parents' guidance on which young men to spend time with.
- ◆ Don't ever marry someone who doesn't have the 100% approval rating of your parents.

6. A Strong Relationship with the Lord Is the Best Spiritual Protection

"Wherefore, my dearly beloved, flee from idolatry."—1 CORINTHIANS 10:14

"Keep thy heart with all diligence; for out of it are the issues of life."—PROVERBS 4:23

"Hear thou, my son, and be wise, and guide thine heart in the way."—PROVERBS 23:19

"This I say then, Walk in the Spirit, and ye shall not fulfil the lust of the flesh."—GALATIANS 5:16

Guard your heart spiritually by spending more time with God than you do with the person in your dating relationship. Make sure that God is first in your life and keep Him there. Walk with Him and determine that you will make Him first in every friendship and dating relationship.

When you begin dating, keep God first and foremost in that friendship. Determine that you will help this other person become a better Christian, and that they will do likewise.

If your dating relationship in any way lessens your heart for God, there is a big problem and it should be stopped immediately.

7. A Strong Relationship with Parents Is the Best Emotional Protection

"The heart is deceitful above all things, and desperately wicked: who can know it?"
—JEREMIAH 17:9

"To keep thee from the evil woman, from the flattery of the tongue of a strange woman."
—PROVERBS 6:24

"Lust not after her beauty in thine heart; neither let her take thee with her eyelids."
—PROVERBS 6:25

Your parents are not only the spiritual protectors in your life, but they are also where you should find your emotional stability. Young people who are close to their parents and godly authorities always have a stronger foundation from which to fight temptation and sin. Those who are not close to their parents are much more susceptible to a wrong kind of friendship or dating relationship.

Your parents should be your best friends! God entrusts them with your life, your heart, and your preparation for the future. Your relationship with them is vital and pivotal to your future. Being close to them gives you an emotional and spiritual strength that is the best resistance against peer pressure and temptation.

The best way to make sure you do not give your heart away prematurely is to stay close to your parents on a weekly and daily basis. Let your parents into your struggles. Share your life with them. Talk with them. Pray with them. Enjoy time with them. Laugh with them. Get their advice. Follow their counsel. They understand you better than anyone!

8. A Strong Commitment to Purity Is the Best Physical Protection

"Flee also youthful lusts: but follow righteousness, faith, charity, peace, with them that call on the Lord out of a pure heart."—2 TIMOTHY 2:22

"Flee fornication. Every sin that a man doeth is without the body; but he that committeth fornication sinneth against his own body." —1 CORINTHIANS 6:18

"A gracious woman retaineth honour: and strong men retain riches."—PROVERBS 11:16

"The elder women as mothers; the younger as sisters, with all purity."—1 TIMOTHY 5:2

"Let no man despise thy youth; but be thou an example of the believers, in word, in conversation, in charity, in spirit, in faith, in purity."—1 TIMOTHY 4:12

This is not the only protection against losing your purity, but it is the best. Surely your pastor, your parents, and other godly authorities will help you to stay pure, but only you can decide to personally make a firm commitment to God that you will protect your purity.

Make a vow before God that you will not become physical in a dating relationship! Determine that you will not be involved in a sexual relationship until marriage, and determine that you won't even begin taking the first steps in that direction by being physical with a guy or a girl.

Make a vow before God that you will never be alone with the opposite sex. Decide that you will always be in sight, with others, and accountable. Do not compromise your physical purity by exposing yourself to temptations physically. Run away, abstain, and determine before God to stay pure!

9. A Wise Person Will Wait until after High School for a Serious Dating Relationship

"Now the end of the commandment is charity out of a pure heart, and of a good conscience, and of faith unfeigned:"—1 TIMOTHY 1:5

If you are a young adult, your priorities do not leave much room for any kind of serious dating relationship. Between family, school, spiritual life, and preparing for your future, dating or having a boyfriend or girlfriend should just be a very low priority. God wants your priorities to be a pure heart, a good conscience, and a real faith—each of these suffer when a dating relationship becomes a priority over more important things.

As a young person, keep a healthy balance in your life. Keep your friendships light and encouraging. Do not become exclusively involved in a dating type of friendship. Have a lot of friends and be friendly. Do not give in to your desires to have that one special person—the risks are too great and it's just not time yet.

Wait until you are closer to marriage to really become interested in a serious dating relationship.

10. Dating Always Poses Risk of Break-up and Disappointment

Be prepared! Most dating relationships come to an end—especially those that happen during the teen years! These early relationships just don't have anywhere to go, and when they end, your heart will be devastated and your life will seem like it's ending along with it. This is one of the best reasons to wait on dating until after teen years.

During a break-up like this, your emotions will be strong and difficult to deal with. It is vital that you remember that these are just emotions. They are powerful emotions but God can give you grace to grow through them! Don't believe them. You do have a future. You do have God. Life will settle down and come back into balance.

Learn the lesson and guard your heart until God brings you the right person at the right time!

Conclusion— The Right Person at the Right Time

Genesis 24 gives us one of the greatest love stories in all the Bible—the coming together of Isaac and Rebekah. There are many principles related to preparing for a future spouse in this story, but here are just a few:

Isaac and Rebekah were focused on living purely before God.

- Rebekah was a pure young lady.
- Rebekah had a servant's heart.

- Rebekah honored her family.
- Isaac loved the Lord and trusted Him.
- Isaac spent time with the Lord and meditated upon His truth.
- Both trusted God for their future spouses.
- Both wanted the will of God more than anything.
- Both trusted their parents and authorities in finding the will of God.
- They fell deeply in love by the will of God (at first sight!).

This story, as few others, reminds us that preparing for a future spouse is not so much about "dating" in the world's sense of the word, as it is about living for God now and trusting Him to intersect your life with the right person at the right time.

More than any emotional attraction, you must protect and prepare your heart for the one spouse whom God is preparing for you. You are preparing now for that lifetime relationship. Honor the Lord in all your relationships now, so that He will honor you in your future marriage!

Questions for Personal Study
Biblical Principles for Dating

1. List some of the key thoughts that you learned from this study.

2. Read the entire chapter of Genesis 24 and see how many life lessons you can write out from that chapter.

3. List as many physical, emotional, and spiritual dangers of premature dating as you can remember.

4. Write out some guidelines that you would desire to set up in your life once you do start dating.

5. Pray right now and ask the Lord to help you guard your heart and life until you meet the right person at the right time.

Godly Leadership
Learning to Rightly Influence Others

"Thus saith the Lord, thy Redeemer, the Holy One of Israel; I am the Lord thy God which teacheth thee to profit, which leadeth thee by the way that thou shouldest go."—Isaiah 48:17

"Let a man so account of us, as of the ministers of Christ, and stewards of the mysteries of God. Moreover it is required in stewards, that a man be found faithful."—1 Corinthians 4:1–2

Everybody Has Influence

Do you remember who the "big kids" were when you were in first grade? Probably the second and third graders! How about when you were in sixth grade? You most likely looked up to the seventh and eight graders. By the time you arrived in junior high, the senior highers were your new role models. And even at the pinnacle of high school—your senior year, you will be looking at college students for influence.

What's the point? Simply this. Everybody is influenced by somebody. Everybody looks up to and follows someone else—which also means that you have influence. You may not see yourself as a leader or as someone who is influential, but this simply is not true. You do have influence and someone is looking at you as a role model.

Consider this question: what kind of influence do you want to be? When you pass other people or when your name comes up at someone's dinner table, what do you want said? What kind of reputation would you like to have? Do you want to be respected, well thought of, and considered highly? Or is it your goal to be seen negatively, to have people try to avoid your influence, or for parents to tell their kids, "Don't be like that person!"?

Deep within, everybody desires a good reputation—the respect of others. Deep inside you want your family and others to be proud of you. You want others to see you positively and to think highly of you. You want people to like you. You would like to be thought of as mature. You would like your name to be associated with good words and a positive reputation.

The amazing news is that, whatever your reputation is right now, you can change it. You may have worked your whole life to establish a good name, and you could lose it in moments. At the same time, you may have made some mistakes and damaged your good name, but there is still an opportunity to rebuild and regain the respect of others. It may take some time and some diligence, but it's well worth it.

This chapter focuses on influence—using your name and reputation to provide spiritual leadership and a godly model for others to follow. No matter what your past is, if you receive these points with an open heart and choose to live them, you will quickly gain a positive reputation and others will quickly begin to grow in respect and admiration of you. Over time, they will begin to see you as a godly leader and a good influence.

You cannot avoid the fact that you are an influence. You can only choose what kind of influence you will be. And one day, you will stand and answer to Jesus Christ for the influence you had on others. Let's take a closer look at how to use our influence to lead others in the right direction.

What God Says about Influence

Leadership is influence, and in the world today there are godly leaders and ungodly leaders. There are those who influence others away from God and righteousness, and those who influence others toward God and righteousness.

You are the steward of your own influence, and God teaches that you will one day give account for how you influenced others in your life. He requires us to be faithful stewards.

Many Christians try to ride the fence on this issue and say that they do not want to influence others. The problem is, there is no middle ground.

Everyone has some measure of influence and everyone uses their influence for right or wrong.

You are a leader in some form or fashion—you cannot escape this fact. You can only decide how you will lead—how you will influence. You must decide what you will do with your influence and how you will steward it.

In the opening verse of this chapter, we see God's heart to teach us, to help us to profit, and to lead us in the way that we should go.

The question of this study is: will you reflect God's heart in the way that you influence others? Will you choose to teach others, help them profit, and show them the right way to go?

A godly person will accept the responsibility of influence and will choose to use it wisely!

Let's consider ten basic characteristics of a person who desires to influence others properly.

1. A Godly Leader Loves and Serves Jesus and Others as a Life Commitment

"And whosoever will be chief among you, let him be your servant:"—MATTHEW 20:27

"But he that is greatest among you shall be your servant."—MATTHEW 23:11

"And he came to Capernaum: and being in the house he asked them, What was it that ye disputed among yourselves by the way? But they held their peace: for by the way they had disputed among themselves, who should be the greatest. And he sat down, and called the twelve, and saith unto them, If any man desire to be first, the same shall be last of all, and servant of all."—MARK 9:33–35

"For we preach not ourselves, but Christ Jesus the Lord; and ourselves your servants for Jesus' sake."—2 CORINTHIANS 4:5

"But made himself of no reputation, and took upon him the form of a servant, and was made in the likeness of men:"—PHILIPPIANS 2:7

"For though I be free from all men, yet have I made myself servant unto all, that I might gain the more."—1 CORINTHIANS 9:19

In both His words and His life, Jesus modeled a kind of leadership that loves other people and serves them. His way of leading was serving. His way "up" is "down." He repeatedly instructs us to serve each other, and even as He washed the disciples' feet, He displayed the heart of a true leader.

Spiritual leadership begins with deciding to love and serve others. A spiritual leader takes on a life commitment—a life paradigm of loving and serving people.

If you desire to lead others in the right direction and have a godly influence on them, do not begin by trying to lead. Begin by serving. Look for ways to love and give yourself to people. Look for needs you can reach out and meet personally. Look for ways to prefer others before yourself.

"Be kindly affectioned one to another with brotherly love; in honour preferring one another;"—ROMANS 12:10

2. A Godly Leader Will Focus on Being a Friend, Not on Having Friends

"A man that hath friends must shew himself friendly: and there is a friend that sticketh closer than a brother."—PROVERBS 18:24

"A friend loveth at all times, and a brother is born for adversity."—PROVERBS 17:17

"Ointment and perfume rejoice the heart: so doth the sweetness of a man's friend by hearty counsel."—PROVERBS 27:9

So many Christians miss this point. We become addicted to having friends and to being liked and accepted! Simply put, being liked isn't all that it's cracked up to be! When you make the goal of your heart to "have friends," suddenly you are chasing the wrong target. You will make decisions and mistakes all based upon the fact that you crave acceptance from others. You will compromise your heart, your integrity, and your vital relationships just for a few people that you think are true friends.

This thinking leads you into a vicious and hurtful cycle of making friends and losing them. You will discover you cannot always keep your "friends" happy, and some who you call friends will actually turn their backs on you and hurt you through gossip or rejection.

There is a better way! You don't have to be led around by peer pressure and weak friendships. You can establish true, godly friendships another way.

Leaders decide that they will be a friend. They change their thinking. They focus on a different goal. Their goal is to be a friend to others and to help meet the needs of others.

In so doing, you will discover that God will give you true friends.

Shift your mentality from having friends to being a friend—you will be amazed at how different and how much better life will become.

3. A Godly Leader Will Hate Sin but Love People and Respect Everybody

"And if any man obey not our word by this epistle, note that man, and have no company with him, that he may be ashamed. Yet count

him not as an enemy, but admonish him as a brother. Now the Lord of peace himself give you peace always by all means. The Lord be with you all."—2 THESSALONIANS 3:14–16

"Brethren, if a man be overtaken in a fault, ye which are spiritual, restore such an one in the spirit of meekness; considering thyself, lest thou also be tempted."—GALATIANS 6:1

"Now we exhort you, brethren, warn them that are unruly, comfort the feebleminded, support the weak, be patient toward all men."—1 THESSALONIANS 5:14

"If it be possible, as much as lieth in you, live peaceably with all men."—ROMANS 12:18

The Bible is clear that we are to use discernment in our Christian relationships. We are to avoid the wrong company and bad influences while at the same time loving and respecting all people. This is sometimes a fine line and a difficult one to learn.

The above verses show us that we are to have a spirit of meekness in restoring others, as well as the courage to separate from a wrong influence without counting that person as an enemy.

Godly leaders will be able to hate the sin and speak against it while at the same time loving the person and admonishing them to choose the right.

Godly leaders do not pick and choose who they will love and who they will reject. As unto the Lord, they see everyone as a life to influence and a person to love.

4. A Godly Leader Will Stand for Right and Doesn't Fear Ridicule

"Yea, and all that will live godly in Christ Jesus shall suffer persecution."—2 TIMOTHY 3:12

"If ye were of the world, the world would love his own: but because ye are not of the world, but I have chosen you out of the world, therefore the world hateth you. Remember the word that I said unto you, The servant is not greater than his lord. If they have persecuted me, they will also persecute you; if they have kept my saying, they will keep yours also. But all these things will they do unto you for my name's sake, because they know not him that sent me."—JOHN 15:19–21

"These things I have spoken unto you, that in me ye might have peace. In the world ye shall have tribulation: but be of good cheer; I have overcome the world." —JOHN 16:33

"That no man should be moved by these afflictions: for yourselves know that we are appointed thereunto."—1 THESSALONIANS 3:3

"For what glory is it, if, when ye be buffeted for your faults, ye shall take it patiently? but if, when ye do well, and suffer for it, ye take it patiently, this is acceptable with God. For even hereunto were ye called: because Christ also suffered for us, leaving us an example, that ye should follow his steps:"—1 PETER 2:20–21

"But and if ye suffer for righteousness' sake, happy are ye: and be not afraid of their terror, neither be troubled;"—1 PETER 3:14

"Beloved, think it not strange concerning the fiery trial which is to try you, as though some strange thing happened unto you: But rejoice, inasmuch as ye are partakers of Christ's sufferings; that, when his glory shall be revealed, ye may be glad also with exceeding joy. If ye be reproached for the name of Christ, happy are ye; for the spirit of glory and of God resteth upon you: on their part he is evil spoken of, but on your part he is glorified."—1 PETER 4:12–14

God teaches that those who live for Him and take a stand will suffer some rejection, persecution, and ridicule. It comes with the territory! Expect it. It's not fun or pleasant, but if you will be a leader, you must be strong enough to "take it."

A godly leader knows, even as he chooses to do right, that he will be rejected. And he decides ahead of time that he can take it! By God's grace, a godly leader isn't surprised or moved by ridicule. In fact, for many, the rejection serves to strengthen their resolve and affirm that they are doing the right thing.

How easily are you moved? How easily do you give in? Do you fear rejection? Do you fear what others might say about you or how they would feel if you did what is right?

God says not to fear these things.

"So that we may boldly say, The Lord is my helper, and I will not fear what man shall do unto me."—HEBREWS 13:6

Decide that you will stand up and be godly, regardless of the ridicule! God will strengthen you and bless you through it—and over time, He will give you great influence because people always want to follow someone who can take some heat!

5. A Godly Leader Finds Success in Helping Others to Grow and Succeed

"Wherefore comfort yourselves together, and edify one another, even as also ye do."
—1 THESSALONIANS 5:11

"All things are lawful for me, but all things are not expedient: all things are lawful for me, but all things edify not."—1 CORINTHIANS 10:23

"Let us therefore follow after the things which make for peace, and things wherewith one may edify another."—ROMANS 14:19

"Let every one of us please his neighbour for his good to edification."—ROMANS 15:2

"But he that prophesieth speaketh unto men to edification, and exhortation, and comfort."
—1 CORINTHIANS 14:3

"We then that are strong ought to bear the infirmities of the weak, and not to please ourselves."—ROMANS 15:1

"Let no man seek his own, but every man another's wealth."—1 CORINTHIANS 10:24

"Even as I please all men in all things, not seeking mine own profit, but the profit of many, that they may be saved."—1 CORINTHIANS 10:33

"Look not every man on his own things, but every man also on the things of others. Let this mind be in you, which was also in Christ Jesus:"—PHILIPPIANS 2:4–5

Each of the above verses shows that the true heart of a godly servant-leader is the benefit and welfare of others. The Bible principle uses the word *edify* or *edification*, which literally means to "build up" or to strengthen.

A godly leader is interested in building others up, while immature Christians and ungodly people are often interested in tearing others down. It's quite simple. Your life, your words, your influence will either build others or hurt them.

Throughout God's Word we are commanded to build up others, to think of them first, to be focused on helping others to succeed and grow. We are to seek others' well-being before our own.

This kind of person helps others be better Christians and looks for ways to help others succeed in life!

One final important thought—godly leaders willingly sacrifice personal rights for the privilege of influencing and helping others, and they believe the trade is well worth it! As you grow in leadership, that influence will mean that you sacrifice some personal rights. What is more important to you—being able to do what you want, or being able to help others?

A godly leader values influence more than personal rights.

6. A Godly Leader Learns How to Communicate Well

"And I beseech you, brethren, suffer the word of exhortation: for I have written a letter unto you in few words."—HEBREWS 13:22

"Ye see how large a letter I have written unto you with mine own hand."—GALATIANS 6:11

This is a simple but important principle. The Apostle Paul is perhaps the best human example we have of this principle. He communicated his heart frequently in both spoken and written words. We will see later in this study that words are powerful, and a godly leader learns how to use words effectively to strengthen and encourage others.

Leaders learn to speak well. They decide to grow in the ability to communicate their words effectively. If you are still a student, take your speech and English classes seriously—they will enable you to better communicate as you grow in leadership.

Leaders learn to write well. They decide to express their true heart in written form—notes, letters, and other forms of communication.

Leaders view all of their communication—written words, spoken words, email, text messages, phone calls, etc. as an opportunity to use the power of words for good. They see every word as a stewardship and every communication as something for which they will answer to God.

Decide that you will learn to communicate effectively in both written and spoken word—God will use that ability to help you influence others towards godliness!

7. A Godly Leader Has a Personal Commitment to Personal Growth

> *"But grow in grace, and in the knowledge of our Lord and Saviour Jesus Christ. To him be glory both now and for ever. Amen."*—2 PETER 3:18

> *"Let the word of Christ dwell in you richly in all wisdom; teaching and admonishing one another in psalms and hymns and spiritual*

songs, singing with grace in your hearts to the Lord."—COLOSSIANS 3:16

"That ye might walk worthy of the Lord unto all pleasing, being fruitful in every good work, and increasing in the knowledge of God;" —COLOSSIANS 1:10

"As newborn babes, desire the sincere milk of the word, that ye may grow thereby:"—1 PETER 2:2

"But the God of all grace, who hath called us unto his eternal glory by Christ Jesus, after that ye have suffered a while, make you perfect, stablish, strengthen, settle you."—1 PETER 5:10

Godly leaders decide that personal growth will be a life-time journey—they choose to be constantly learning, stretching, and progressing forward on every level.

As a result, Bible knowledge, wisdom, and understanding become a life-long pursuit. A godly leader never stops desiring to grow, to reach his potential, and to enlarge his capacity for the Lord.

A godly leader makes the following things a regular priority in his life:

+ Bible reading, study, meditation, and memorization
+ Reading biographies of great lives and Christians
+ Reading Christian books with a biblical message
+ Listening to godly music that edifies the heart
+ Listening to preaching and teaching both at church and privately
+ Participating in growth-oriented activities—camps, conferences, etc.

Godly leaders value growth more than they value personal pleasure or fun. For a leader, growth is fun. A leader gives his mind and heart to strengthening influences not depleting ones.

Depleting influences include:

- Excessive TV watching
- Excessive video game playing
- Excessive movie watching
- The world's music
- The world's friendships
- The world's entertainment forms

Strengthening influences include:

- Bible reading and study
- Private prayer
- Godly Christian music
- Sermons and lessons
- Christian books and biographies
- Christian retreats, camps, and conferences
- Godly friendships

What do you do with the extra time you have available in a week? Do you vegetate or do you grow? It is your choice, but leaders choose to grow!

8. A Godly Leader Learns to Live a Well Ordered and Balanced Life

"Let all things be done decently and in order."
—1 CORINTHIANS 14:40

"For this cause left I thee in Crete, that thou shouldest set in order the things that are wanting,

and ordain elders in every city, as I had appointed thee:"—TITUS 1:5

"And if any man hunger, let him eat at home; that ye come not together unto condemnation. And the rest will I set in order when I come." —1 CORINTHIANS 11:34

"For God is not the author of confusion, but of peace, as in all churches of the saints." —1 CORINTHIANS 14:33

"A false balance is abomination to the LORD: but a just weight is his delight."—PROVERBS 11:1

Simply put, leaders lead themselves first. They learn how to bring order and organization to their lives through personal discipline, and they learn to lead balanced lives (bringing the right order and time to their life priorities).

Personal organization reflects the character of God in your life. He is a God of order. His creation shows order. And He desires for us to lead orderly lives.

How does this matter to a young adult? As a young person, learning to have an orderly bedroom, and organized desk or locker, and a clean car shows a growing character in your life.

Bringing order to the details of your life shows personal discipline that will allow you greater influence. Don't be content with a disorderly closet or room. Don't walk by a junk drawer. Decide that you will develop a character that reflects God's order in each of these small areas of your life.

As your life has order and balance, you will be able to have a greater influence on others.

9. A Godly Leader Cares about a Good Name and Godly Testimony

"A good name is rather to be chosen than great riches, and loving favour rather than silver and gold."—Proverbs 22:1

"A good name is better than precious ointment; and the day of death than the day of one's birth."—Ecclesiastes 7:1

"Wherefore, brethren, look ye out among you seven men of honest report, full of the Holy Ghost and wisdom, whom we may appoint over this business."—Acts 6:3

"And one Ananias, a devout man according to the law, having a good report of all the Jews which dwelt there," —Acts 22:12

"Demetrius hath good report of all men, and of the truth itself: yea, and we also bear record; and ye know that our record is true."—3 John 12

We have spent much time in earlier chapters talking about the importance of a godly testimony in our outward lifestyle.

The Bible instructs us to have a "good name" and tells us of men who have a "good report"! This should be your desire as well.

Godly leaders value what others think of them as unto the Lord. It is not about vanity or popularity. It is about a desire to honor and glorify the Lord in all things.

In relation to leadership, this is about influencing others to honor God in the same way!

Godly leaders choose to abstain from the appearance of evil in order to protect their privilege to influence others.

10. A Godly Leader Is Destination Oriented for Himself and Others

"Not as though I had already attained, either were already perfect: but I follow after, if that I may apprehend that for which also I am apprehended of Christ Jesus. Brethren, I count not myself to have apprehended: but this one thing I do, forgetting those things which are behind, and reaching forth unto those things which are before, I press toward the mark for the prize of the high calling of God in Christ Jesus."—PHILIPPIANS 3:12–14

"Only let your conversation be as it becometh the gospel of Christ: that whether I come and see you, or else be absent, I may hear of your affairs, that ye stand fast in one spirit, with one mind striving together for the faith of the gospel;"—PHILIPPIANS 1:27

"I have fought a good fight, I have finished my course, I have kept the faith:"—2 TIMOTHY 4:7

"Wherefore seeing we also are compassed about with so great a cloud of witnesses, let us lay aside every weight, and the sin which doth so easily beset us, and let us run with patience the race that is set before us,"—HEBREWS 12:1

"And let us not be weary in well doing: for in due season we shall reap, if we faint not." —GALATIANS 6:9

"Know ye not that they which run in a race run all, but one receiveth the prize? So run, that ye may obtain." —1 CORINTHIANS 9:24

"Whether therefore ye eat, or drink, or whatsoever ye do, do all to the glory of God." —1 CORINTHIANS 10:31

A godly leader has a life pursuit! He understands that God has given him a high calling, and he passionately and faithfully embraces that calling and pursues it with all of his might for the glory of God.

A godly leader sees and lives with the destination in mind. He is not distracted by pettiness, gossip, and meaningless living. He has his eye on a prize and runs passionately toward that prize until the Lord calls him home.

A godly leader is also focused on helping others run their race well for the Lord.

Conclusion

We have seen ten attributes of godly leadership. We have seen that you have influence whether you want it or not. Decide that you will be a good steward of the influence that God has given you.

There is great joy and happiness in helping others succeed—in serving others and having their best interests at heart! God blesses this kind of leader.

Choose to be a godly leader today!

Questions for Personal Study
Godly Leadership

1. What is your natural response to leadership—do you tend to seek it or run from it?

2. Which points of this study spoke the most to your heart and why?

3. What are some ways that you've been avoiding leadership where you know God wants you to take a stand?

4. What are the results of situations and circumstances where people refuse to lead or have a godly influence?

5. Pray right now and ask the Lord to help you use your influence in a godly way.

CHAPTER ELEVEN

Interpersonal Communications

Using My Words to Honor Jesus Christ
and Encourage Others

"For in many things we offend all. If any man offend not in word, the same is a perfect man, and able also to bridle the whole body. Behold, we put bits in the horses' mouths, that they may obey us; and we turn about their whole body. Behold also the ships, which though they be so great, and are driven of fierce winds, yet are they turned about with a very small helm, whithersoever the governor listeth. Even so the tongue is a little member, and boasteth great things. Behold, how great a matter a little fire kindleth! And the tongue is a fire, a world of iniquity: so is the tongue among our members, that it defileth the whole body, and setteth on fire the course of nature; and it is set on fire of hell. For every kind of beasts, and of birds, and of serpents, and of things in the sea, is tamed, and hath been tamed of mankind: But the tongue can no man tame; it is an unruly evil, full of deadly poison. Therewith bless we God, even the Father; and therewith curse we men, which are made after the similitude of God. Out of the same mouth proceedeth

blessing and cursing. My brethren, these things ought not so to be. Doth a fountain send forth at the same place sweet water and bitter? Can the fig tree, my brethren, bear olive berries? either a vine, figs? so can no fountain both yield salt water and fresh. Who is a wise man and endued with knowledge among you? let him shew out of a good conversation his works with meekness of wisdom."—JAMES 3:2–13

The Amazing Power of Words

If there were a lunatic on your street randomly shooting a gun or a hunting bow with razor sharp arrows, what would you do? Run? Duck? Hide? All three? If you had half a brain, you would do everything within your power to get out of the way! Why? Because these things destroy. They inflict a lot of pain and damage.

Interestingly, the Bible compares our words to arrows! Jeremiah 9:8 says, *"Their tongue is as an arrow shot out; it speaketh deceit: one speaketh peaceably to his neighbour with his mouth, but in heart he layeth his wait."* Proverbs 25:18 says, *"A man that beareth false witness against his neighbour is a maul, and a sword, and a sharp arrow."*

Maybe you never thought of yourself as a random shooter, but your words are like powerful bullets or arrows! They always hit someone and they always have an impact. Are you a drive-by shooter when it comes to your words? Are you carefully aiming well-chosen words at specific targets for a specific purpose, or are you dangerously using words with no thought of their impact?

An arrow or a bullet can be used for both good and bad. When aimed at the right target, an arrow can provide meat for a hungry family or protection from a wild animal. But, when used randomly, an arrow can do a lot of destruction and cause a lot of pain.

Even so, your words either inflict hurt and pain, or they provide help and encouragement. It's one of the two! Your words always have an impact—all of your words, even the ones you write, text, email, or type! Every word you communicate flows directly from your heart to impact the hearts of others. Words are always powerful—either for good or bad.

One day, when life is over, you will give an account for every word. Matthew 12:36 says, *"But I say unto you, that every idle word that men shall speak, they shall give account thereof in the day of judgment."* Think of that. Every single word that came from your mouth will be accounted for when you face Jesus Christ. That is how much words matter to God! How powerful and important are our communications!

In this chapter, we will see that the Bible has much to say about the things we say and the ways we communicate! You probably haven't given this power a second thought. So, open your heart and listen to what God says about the power of words. Don't be a random shooter. Your tongue is like a bow— be sure to select your targets carefully, and use your arrows for good!

What God Says about Words

There are literally thousands of verses and passages of Scripture that deal with our communications. God makes it abundantly clear that our words, our lips, our conversation, and our communications matter greatly to Him and to His purposes. It would be impossible to do an exhaustive study of this subject in one short study because the Bible speaks so powerfully about it. In the coming pages, we will see a brief overview of God's plan for our communications—our words.

Jesus is our ultimate example and model of how to use our words to please the Lord. He never sinned one time, and His words were always exactly what His Heavenly Father intended. Notice how Jesus spoke:

Jesus spoke graciously:

> *"And all bare him witness, and wondered at the gracious words which proceeded out of his mouth. And they said, Is not this Joseph's son?"*—LUKE 4:22

Jesus spoke differently than other men:

> *"The officers answered, Never man spake like this man."*—JOHN 7:46

Jesus used His words to teach others, based upon the authority of God's truth:

> *"And they were astonished at his doctrine: for he taught them as one that had authority, and not as the scribes."*—MARK 1:22

God has given you the ability to speak, to write, to communicate with words to others. He has a purpose for your words, and part of growing in maturity as a godly person involves learning how to use your words for God's glory.

Let's discover the power and the purpose of our words!

1. God Created Communication, but Man Perverts It and Uses It Sinfully

> *"And the whole earth was of one language, and of one speech. And it came to pass, as they journeyed from the east, that they found a*

plain in the land of Shinar; and they dwelt there. And they said one to another, Go to, let us make brick, and burn them throughly. And they had brick for stone, and slime had they for morter. And they said, Go to, let us build us a city and a tower, whose top may reach unto heaven; and let us make us a name, lest we be scattered abroad upon the face of the whole earth. And the LORD came down to see the city and the tower, which the children of men builded. And the LORD said, Behold, the people is one, and they have all one language; and this they begin to do: and now nothing will be restrained from them, which they have imagined to do. Go to, let us go down, and there confound their language, that they may not understand one another's speech. So the LORD scattered them abroad from thence upon the face of all the earth: and they left off to build the city. Therefore is the name of it called Babel; because the LORD did there confound the language of all the earth: and from thence did the LORD scatter them abroad upon the face of all the earth."—GENESIS 11:1–9

In the above passage, mankind had taken language and imagination to new depths of depravity and wickedness. They so perverted God's gift of communication that God decided to confound their ability to communicate. He decided to limit mankind by limiting their ability to communicate with each other.

It is obvious that man perverted God's intended purpose for language and communication.

Our world today has not changed much since that time. We live in a day when mankind is filled with wicked imaginations and filthy communications. We live in a day when those wicked communications are flowing constantly on TV, in movies, in books, in magazines, on computers, on cell phones, and on the lips of lost men. Men seem to be bent on perverted communications.

You must realize that when you participate in filthy communication, you are displeasing God and abusing His purpose for your words.

2. God's Purpose for Communication Is His Glory and the Edification of Others

Why did God originally give men the ability to communicate? For what purpose did He create languages, words, and methods of communicating?

God gave communication skills to His creatures for two basic purposes:

The first purpose of all communication is to glorify God.

> *"That ye may with one mind and one mouth glorify God, even the Father of our Lord Jesus Christ."*—ROMANS 15:6

> *"I will praise thee, O Lord my God, with all my heart: and I will glorify thy name for evermore."*—PSALM 86:12

> *"O Lord, open thou my lips; and my mouth shall shew forth thy praise."*—PSALM 51:15

> *"Because thy lovingkindness is better than life, my lips shall praise thee."*—PSALM 63:3

The word *glorify* means "to make glorious or to magnify or enlarge." Our responsibility in all communication is to make God look better!

Every kind of communication that flows from our hearts should uplift Jesus Christ and make His name better and well known before others. For this reason, every kind of communication—every form of words that flow from our thoughts, should be carefully purposed and premeditated!

The second purpose of all communication is to edify others.

> *"Let no corrupt communication proceed out of your mouth, but that which is good to the use of edifying, that it may minister grace unto the hearers. And grieve not the holy Spirit of God, whereby ye are sealed unto the day of redemption. Let all bitterness, and wrath, and anger, and clamour, and evil speaking, be put away from you, with all malice: And be ye kind one to another, tenderhearted, forgiving one another, even as God for Christ's sake hath forgiven you."*—EPHESIANS 4:29–32

> *"Let us therefore follow after the things which make for peace, and things wherewith one may edify another."*—ROMANS 14:19

The word *edify* means "to purposefully cause someone to go forward or to build up." Our words have the power to benefit others and encourage growth!

Most communications glorify self and minimize others. Too often we are self-centered in our communication, and we become involved in gossip and hurtful talk. But a mature Christian realizes that all communication was designed by God to glorify Him and edify others.

When it comes to speaking, writing, texting, emailing, or communicating in any form, remember these two critical phrases: **glorify God, edify others!**

We do not belong to ourselves. We do not have the right to use our thoughts, our tongues, or our words in a way that does not fulfill God's purposes!

> *"Their throat is an open sepulchre; with their tongues they have used deceit; the poison of asps is under their lips: Whose mouth is full of cursing and bitterness."*—ROMANS 3:13–14

3. Words Carry an Extreme Power for Good or for Bad

> *"Death and life are in the power of the tongue: and they that love it shall eat the fruit thereof."*—PROVERBS 18:21

> *"Not that which goeth into the mouth defileth a man; but that which cometh out of the mouth, this defileth a man."*—MATTHEW 15:11

Have you ever stopped to consider the power of words? God designed words to have great power—especially written words! Think about the above verses—the tongue has the power of life and death! The tongue has the power to defile!

Have you ever considered that God gave us a written Word because words are so powerful? Having God's written Word is better than seeing Him in person! How? Simply this. When someone puts something in writing, you are able to read their heart and thoughts in print. But if you simply see a person, you cannot understand their heart. Rather than see God, you get to read His heart every time you open His Word.

Think of it this way. If you have an interest or a love for someone, what is one of the first things you look for from that person? A note. When finally you send a note or receive a note, you suddenly have a written expression of the heart. You read that note with great interest. You save it, re-read it, and study it! Why? Because written words are the powerful expression of the inner heart.

In the same way, all of your words have great power—power to build up or to destroy. And a wise Christian will place great weight and value upon the power of words. Choose to use your words wisely. Choose to use your words for good.

4. God Commands Us to Avoid All Corrupt Communication

God describes bad communications in the verses below. As a Christian, you will be tempted every day through peer pressure and media to participate in or to laugh at corrupt communication. Think about what God says about these perverse kinds of communications:

> "Let no corrupt communication proceed out of your mouth, but that which is good to the use of edifying, that it may minister grace unto the hearers."—EPHESIANS 4:29

> "Put away from thee a froward mouth, and perverse lips put far from thee."—PROVERBS 4:24

> "But fornication, and all uncleanness, or covetousness, let it not be once named among you,

*as becometh saints; Neither filthiness, nor foolish
talking, nor jesting, which are not convenient: but
rather giving of thanks."*—EPHESIANS 5:3–4

*"But now ye also put off all these; anger, wrath,
malice, blasphemy, filthy communication out
of your mouth. Lie not one to another, seeing
that ye have put off the old man with his deeds;"*
—COLOSSIANS 3:8–9

The word *corrupt* literally means "rotten" or "worthless."
The word *filthy* means "vile" or "shameful." Over and over
in these verses we are commanded to put away, put off, and
avoid all types of sinful communication. God even addresses
our joking and our humor. Yes, God is even concerned that
you learn to laugh at the right things.

One of the most powerful signs of maturity is your
ability to communicate well and to abstain from corrupt
communication. Decide now that you will not be enamored
by words that you know displease the Lord.

Decide that you will honor the maker of your
tongue—the God of your heart! When you are around
corrupt communication, you must do one of several
things immediately:

Right Responses to Corrupt Communication with People

1. Walk away or leave.
2. Refuse to laugh.
3. Take a stand by asking someone to stop.
4. Give up these friends and choose more godly friends.
5. Speak to someone in authority about the problem.
6. Encourage others to walk away.

7. Ask God to cleanse your mind immediately.

Right Responses to Corrupt Communication in Places of Business

1. Leave. Eat or shop somewhere else.
2. Ask management to turn the music down or TV off.
3. Choose a seat or location as far away as possible from the source.
4. Speak to a manager or write a letter to corporate headquarters.
5. Seek to avoid this place in the future.
6. Use Scripture or prayer to focus your heart elsewhere.
7. Ask God to cleanse your mind immediately.

Right Responses to Corrupt Communication in Media

1. Turn it off.
2. Turn it down.
3. Change the channel.
4. Invest your time into godly influences.
5. Determine to value your heart more than you value entertainment.

5. Corrupt Communication Creates Deep Spiritual Damage to the Heart

"The wicked is snared by the transgression of his lips: but the just shall come out of trouble."
—Proverbs 12:13

*"The tongue of the wise useth knowledge aright:
but the mouth of fools poureth out foolishness.
The eyes of the* LORD *are in every place,
beholding the evil and the good. A wholesome
tongue is a tree of life: but perverseness therein
is a breach in the spirit."*—PROVERBS 15:2–4

*"The words of a wise man's mouth are gracious;
but the lips of a fool will swallow up himself."*
—ECCLESIASTES 10:12

*"Be not deceived: evil communications corrupt
good manners."*—1 CORINTHIANS 15:33

The word *breach* in Proverbs 15:4 literally means "a fracture or a brokenness that leads to ruin." God is saying that our communications not only impact others, but they impact our inner man as well! Your words affect you! When you participate in corrupt communications, you are eroding your own heart and spiritual health.

The verse above from 1 Corinthians says that evil communications *corrupt*—which means to cause something to shrivel up and die. *Good manners* refers to moral habits or a godly lifestyle. In other words, if you desire to stay strong and spiritually healthy by God's grace, it will partially involve how you communicate!

To put it simply, sinful communication will do as much damage to yourself as to others! For this reason we are commanded to "keep thy heart"—to guard our hearts from theses kinds of influences. Like a tree that is eroding from the inside out, or a house that is being eaten by termites within, eventually the inner damage will cause your life to collapse in ruin.

One of the best reasons to choose wholesome words and godly speech is to protect your own heart!

6. God Desires to Control Our Words and to Use Our Communications for Good and for Edification

"Set a watch, O Lord, before my mouth; keep the door of my lips."—Psalm 141:3

"A word fitly spoken is like apples of gold in pictures of silver."—Proverbs 25:11

"The Lord God hath given me the tongue of the learned, that I should know how to speak a word in season to him that is weary: he wakeneth morning by morning, he wakeneth mine ear to hear as the learned."—Isaiah 50:4

"I said, I will take heed to my ways, that I sin not with my tongue: I will keep my mouth with a bridle, while the wicked is before me."
—Psalm 39:1

In the above verses we see the key to having good communications!

Godly communication is a result of the controlling power of God. As you yield your thoughts, your tongue, and your communication to the Lord, He will guide your heart and help you say good things that glorify Him and edify others.

God has given you the ability to communicate. Furthermore, He has saved you and redeemed you to Himself. You belong to Him. You are His ambassador. You are His vessel. Your heart, your thoughts, your tongue, and your ability to communicate all belong to Him.

It is reasonable that each morning you would wake up and present yourself as a living sacrifice to the Lord. Decide to start each day by surrendering all of your communicative ability to God. Ask Him to fill you, to control you, to guide your words. Ask Him to "keep the door of your lips." Ask Him to help you choose words that glorify Him and edify others!

Decide that you will not be a gossip. Decide that you will not participate in filthy talking or joking. Decide that you will not listen to or hang around evil communication. Choose to be God's vessel, His messenger. See each day as your assignment from God. Recognize that He has a message He wants you to communicate in every circumstance and every life setting. Realize that His Holy Spirit has specific things that you should say as you represent Him each moment.

Decide to be God's mouthpiece to your friends, your family, your community, and your world!

Ask God to control every word that comes from your being and to make each word something that pleases Him!

7. Communication Has Never Been as Convenient and Technological as It Is Today

"All the words of my mouth are in righteousness; there is nothing froward or perverse in them."
—PROVERBS 8:8

"My heart is inditing a good matter: I speak of the things which I have made touching the king: my tongue is the pen of a ready writer."—PSALM 45:1

The writer of Proverbs 8:8 referenced "all the words." The psalmist in Psalm 45 compares the written word to the tongue. The point is this, God is interested in every word that we communicate—whether spoken or written.

We live in the information age! Communication has never been faster or easier. Words fly back and forth around the globe at the speed of light! We use our computers, email, cell phones, and even gaming systems and music players to communicate to others.

All of this techno-culture has given us a new world of potential to communicate for good or for bad! Unfortunately, Satan has prevented many Christians from using technology for good communication, and he has actually used many technologies to tempt Christians and to ensnare them into ungodly communications.

In today's culture, people will say in a chat room, text message, or email, things that they would never say in person or write in their own handwriting. Many people are addicted to being "online"—they have created artificial identities, second lives, and internet relationships that are eroding and destroying their real life. Rather than using technology wisely, we are using it to our own destruction!

All of this convenience presents today's Christian with a new world of choices and options when it comes to communication. You must be aware of the dangers and deliberately choose to do right in a world that is working hard to destroy you.

Satan's traps are subtler than ever, so you must protect yourself on purpose!

8. A Wise Christian Will Learn to Use Technology to Create and Spread Godly Communication

"Heaviness in the heart of man maketh it stoop: but a good word maketh it glad."—PROVERBS 12:25

"A man hath joy by the answer of his mouth: and a word spoken in due season, how good is it!"—PROVERBS 15:23

"Let us therefore follow after the things which make for peace, and things wherewith one may edify another."—ROMANS 14:19

"Let every one of us please his neighbour for his good to edification."—ROMANS 15:2

"Again, think ye that we excuse ourselves unto you? we speak before God in Christ: but we do all things, dearly beloved, for your edifying."—2 CORINTHIANS 12:19

"Let your speech be alway with grace, seasoned with salt, that ye may know how ye ought to answer every man."—COLOSSIANS 4:6

Again, these verses challenge us to allow all of our communications at all times to be pleasing to the Lord and edifying to others! Are you starting to see God's priorities? He wants every word, every note, every email, every text, every internet posting, every communication to be glorifying and edifying!

In today's culture, people often use technology to spread gossip, to communicate inappropriately, and to dishonor the Lord. A godly person will see every communication as an opportunity to please Christ!

Here are a few guidelines for guarding your life and using techno-communications wisely:

First, stay accountable. Make sure that your family and godly people have access to your email, your cell phone, and your other forms of communication. This will help you avoid temptation and help your godly authorities fight the battle with you. Satan desires to draw you into "secret" communication where he can trap you. Decide that you will not allow him to do this.

Second, stay truthful. Decide that you will not participate in false identities and techno-gossip. Chat rooms, blogs, text messaging, and email often lend in the youth culture to lies and deception. Decide to stay away from social networking sites. Decide that you will be you all the time! Decide that the things you read and write will be true and godly.

Third, stay helpful. There are a lot of "interesting things" online or in techno-communications that really are not helpful. They may be entertaining, fun, or interesting, but for your heart, they simply distract you from something more meaningful or important. Decide that your communications in the world of technology will be focused on that which is helpful and edifying!

Fourth, stay purposeful. Decide that you will use technology for a purpose, not merely to waste time or to fill idle time. Modern communications offer too many inroads to sin and corruption, and it is vital that you decide to use technology for a purpose that pleases God. When you go online, let it be for a specific reason. Don't surf. When you send a text or email, let it be to communicate a specific message. Don't merely throw words around because you have nothing better to do.

9. Good Communication Establishes a Good Name and a Godly Reputation

The truth is, there is great reward in becoming a godly and edifying communicator! People respect someone and trust someone who can control their tongue—someone who values the power of words.

Look at what the Bible says about those who are wise with their words:

First, godly communicators are listened to and respected.

> "*The words of wise men are heard in quiet more than the cry of him that ruleth among fools.*"
> —Ecclesiastes 9:17

Second, godly communicators find a strong footing in life and don't "slide" into problems as easily.

> "*The mouth of the righteous speaketh wisdom, and his tongue talketh of judgment. The law of his God is in his heart; none of his steps shall slide.*"—Psalm 37:30–31

Third, godly communicators are spoken of highly by others.

> "*The wise in heart shall be called prudent: and the sweetness of the lips increaseth learning.*"
> —Proverbs 16:21

Fourth, godly communicators are not legitimately evil-spoken of by others.

> "*Sound speech, that cannot be condemned; that he that is of the contrary part may be ashamed, having no evil thing to say of you.*"—Titus 2:8

The lessons here show us that our words form a large part of our reputation! Choosing your words carefully and making sure your communications are godly will ultimately benefit you as much as anyone else!

Do you have a bad name? Do you have a rough past or a tarnished reputation? If so, you might find that it is the result of your words. Before you blame others, take inventory of what you say or write. Think about how you communicate. Your reputation is greatly impacted by your communication.

Therefore, the best way to establish a good name is to start communicating good things frequently!

10. Godly Communication Focuses on Sharing God's Truth with Others

God wants His truth to be on our minds and on our lips! Notice His command to Joshua and then the following verses that command us to speak and teach God's truth:

> *"This book of the law shall not depart out of thy mouth; but thou shalt meditate therein day and night, that thou mayest observe to do according to all that is written therein: for then thou shalt make thy way prosperous, and then thou shalt have good success."*—JOSHUA 1:8

> *"My tongue shall speak of thy word: for all thy commandments are righteousness."*—PSALM 119:172

> *"Go ye therefore, and teach all nations, baptizing them in the name of the Father, and of the Son, and of the Holy Ghost:"*—MATTHEW 28:19

> *"But ye shall receive power, after that the Holy Ghost is come upon you: and ye shall be witnesses unto me both in Jerusalem, and in all Judaea, and in Samaria, and unto the uttermost part of the earth."*—ACTS 1:8

If we took every word you spoke or wrote last week, what percentage of those words would glorify God and edify others? What percentage of those words would include speaking or teaching God's truth to others?

If you would like to harness the power of your words and make sure that what you say pleases God and helps others, then focus your words on God's Word! Share God's Word, witness to the lost, and encourage others with biblical principles. Look at every circumstance and human interaction as a potential intersection with biblical truth! View each communication as a chance to say something true, biblical, and godly.

You will be shocked how often you can encourage and edify others by referring them to a principle or promise from God's Word. You will be amazed how God will use your words to edify others and glorify Himself. People would come to think of you as "a wise encourager"! That is certainly a better reputation than "the local gossip."

Conclusion

> *"For I will give you a mouth and wisdom, which all your adversaries shall not be able to gainsay nor resist."*—LUKE 21:15

Are you beginning to understand the amazing power of words? Do you see how important your words are to God and to others?

May your prayer be that of Proverbs 8:6–7:

> *"Hear; for I will speak of excellent things; and the opening of my lips shall be right things. For my mouth shall speak truth; and wickedness is an abomination to my lips."*—PROVERBS 8:6–7

Ask God to help you speak of those things that are excellent in the sight of God! Ask Him to make you an edifying communicator for His glory!

Questions for Personal Study
Interpersonal Communications

1. In what ways did God speak to your heart and life through this study?

2. List the primary ways you communicate with others in your daily life.

3. Describe a recent time when you used words in a way that dishonored the Lord. What was the result?

4. Ask the Lord if there is anyone whom you have hurt with your words. Determine today to make your heart right with that person.

5. Write out and memorize Proverbs 8:6–7 about excellent communication.

CHAPTER TWELVE

Conclusion
Growing in God's Grace Day by Day

"Wherefore laying aside all malice, and all guile, and hypocrisies, and envies, and all evil speakings, As newborn babes, desire the sincere milk of the word, that ye may grow thereby: If so be ye have tasted that the Lord is gracious."—1 PETER 2:1–3

"But grow in grace, and in the knowledge of our Lord and Saviour Jesus Christ. To him be glory both now and for ever. Amen."—2 PETER 3:18

A Godly Lifestyle in Perspective

As we conclude this study we have covered a lot of ground! We have seen a lot of Scriptures that teach God's heart and plan for our outward lifestyle!

God is truly interested in a lifestyle that pleases Him, but it must also flow from a heart that loves Him. Take a moment and review the things we've discovered about a godly lifestyle.

Chapters Two and Three: God Created Men and Women Differently and with Different Purposes

"So God created man in his own image, in the image of God created he him; male and female created he them."—GENESIS 1:27

"Male and female created he them; and blessed them, and called their name Adam, in the day when they were created."—GENESIS 5:2

Chapter Four: God Desires for My Clothing to Reflect Him Appropriately in My Life

"But ye are a chosen generation, a royal priesthood, an holy nation, a peculiar people; that ye should shew forth the praises of him who hath called you out of darkness into his marvellous light:"—1 PETER 2:9

"...for man looketh on the outward appearance..."—1 SAMUEL 16:7

"Let your light so shine before men, that they may see your good works, and glorify your Father which is in heaven."—MATTHEW 5:16

Chapter Five: God's Word Teaches That My Behavior Is a Reflection of My Heart for God

"I will behave myself wisely in a perfect way. O when wilt thou come unto me? I will walk within my house with a perfect heart."
—PSALM 101:2

"And be not conformed to this world: but be ye transformed by the renewing of your mind, that ye may prove what is that good, and acceptable, and perfect, will of God."—ROMANS 12:2

Chapter Six: A Godly Lifestyle Includes a Godly Appearance and Caring for My Body

"For ye are bought with a price: therefore glorify God in your body, and in your spirit, which are God's."—1 CORINTHIANS 6:20

"I speak after the manner of men because of the infirmity of your flesh: for as ye have yielded your members servants to uncleanness and to iniquity unto iniquity; even so now yield your members servants to righteousness unto holiness."—ROMANS 6:19

"I beseech you therefore, brethren, by the mercies of God, that ye present your bodies a living sacrifice, holy, acceptable unto God, which is your reasonable service."—ROMANS 12:1

Chapter Seven: God's Blessing and Favour Is Promised to Those under His Plan for Authority

"Let every soul be subject unto the higher powers. For there is no power but of God: the powers that be are ordained of God."—ROMANS 13:1

"Honour thy father and thy mother, as the LORD thy God hath commanded thee; that thy days may be prolonged, and that it may go well with thee, in the land which the LORD thy God giveth thee."—DEUTERONOMY 5:16

Chapter Eight: God Desires for Me to Honor Him through Every Earthly Relationship

"Let all bitterness, and wrath, and anger, and clamour, and evil speaking, be put away from you, with all malice: And be ye kind one to another, tenderhearted, forgiving one another, even as God for Christ's sake hath forgiven you."—EPHESIANS 4:31–32

"Be kindly affectioned one to another with brotherly love; in honour preferring one another;"—ROMANS 12:10

Chapter Nine: God Desires to Prepare My Life for the Right Person at the Right Time

"Keep thy heart with all diligence; for out of it are the issues of life." —PROVERBS 4:23

"Flee also youthful lusts: but follow righteousness, faith, charity, peace, with them that call on the Lord out of a pure heart."—2 TIMOTHY 2:22

Chapter Ten: A Godly Life Involves Leading and Influencing Other People towards God

"Now we exhort you, brethren, warn them that are unruly, comfort the feebleminded, support the weak, be patient toward all men."
—1 THESSALONIANS 5:14

"Let every one of us please his neighbour for his good to edification."—ROMANS 15:2

Chapter Eleven: A Godly Person Chooses to Use Words to Glorify God and Edify Others

"Let no corrupt communication proceed out of your mouth, but that which is good to the use of edifying, that it may minister grace unto the hearers. And grieve not the holy Spirit of God, whereby ye are sealed unto the day of redemption. Let all bitterness, and wrath, and anger, and clamour, and evil speaking, be put away from you, with all malice: And be ye kind one to another, tenderhearted, forgiving one another, even as God for Christ's sake hath forgiven you."—EPHESIANS 4:29–32

Conclusion—Embracing God's Way

As you set this study down, I want to close with a few important thoughts.

First, living a godly lifestyle begins in your heart attitude and then flows into your outward behavior. Remember, God isn't merely interested in outward conformity. He desires for you to willingly, gladly, and joyfully embrace the changes that He has set forth in His Word. He commands us to be different, but He wants us to do so with sincerely submitted hearts.

Putting this lifestyle "on" will seem restricting, imposing, and it will go against your self-will or your nature. You might have heard someone say, "Well, that's just not who I am!" or "I disagree, because I don't think that way…I don't want to live that way…and God loves me just as I am for who I am." Sure, God does love you just as you are for who you are, and that will never change. The question is not: does God love you? The question is: do you love Him enough to please Him—to live life the way He has clearly stated He desires it to be lived? Do you love Him enough to change the way you live as He transforms you into the image of His Son?

Satan might tempt you to think that this lifestyle is "restrictive" or that it infringes on your freedom. But that's just a lie. A godly lifestyle is a delightfully, wonderfully different kind of life! At first, it will boil down to a battle of your will against God's. In other words, you will wrestle with what you want to do versus what God says He desires. You will even be tempted to rationalize and reason that your behavior doesn't matter to God so long as you feel warm and fuzzy about Him in your heart.

Friend, a godly lifestyle is not only biblical, but it is joyful! It is good! What little sacrifice it requires in your personal preferences, God repays ten fold in the blessings of life! It's not the godly lifestyle that is restrictive or oppressive—but rather it's the attitude of your heart. You can embrace God's plan or resist it. It's not the plan itself that is frustrating, it is your attitude towards it, and towards God.

You could decide right now to embrace this life joyfully and willingly, and immediately God would begin a supernatural work in your heart to replace your desires and grow your godly life from the inside out! God will do the work, but you must make the choice to submit—to embrace His desires with a right attitude.

I challenge you in your Christian life—stop asking the wrong questions. Too often Christians ask, "How far can I go without getting hurt? How much can I do? What can I get away with? How close to the line will God allow me to live?"

These are the wrong questions. Rather, we should simply ask, "What is the most pleasing and glorifying to God? In this situation, which path is the holiest, the wisest, the godliest, and the most honoring to my Saviour?"

This heart and spirit is not only pleasing to God, it does something supernatural. It places your life into the transforming hands of God! This attitude of the heart enables God to literally change the way you think and who you are in your heart. I promise, you won't miss your old life for very long! Within a short time, you will begin to experience God's change in your heart, and you will truly taste the delight and blessedness of living God's way!

Finally, it is vital that you remember God's plan for changing your life! We have studied a lot of things that God wants us to "do" or "be" but He does not require you to manufacture all the change in your own strength! God promises that He will produce the change if you will allow Him! It is His power and His strength that will change you from the inside out. It is His touch that will change your heart's desires as well as your outward lifestyle.

If you determine to make all of these changes happen in your own strength, you will end up frustrated and discouraged. Yet, if you yield your heart and life to Jesus Christ, with a good attitude, you will embark on a delightful, life-long journey of growth in God's grace that will bring about true change little by little, day by day.

Consider God's promises in these Scriptures and begin to depend upon His power and His strength to change you and grow you in His grace day by day!

> *"For it is God which worketh in you both to will and to do of his good pleasure."*—PHILIPPIANS 2:13

> *"But the God of all grace, who hath called us unto his eternal glory by Christ Jesus, after that ye have suffered a while, make you perfect, stablish, strengthen, settle you."*—1 PETER 5:10

> *"Being confident of this very thing, that he which hath begun a good work in you will perform it until the day of Jesus Christ:"*—PHILIPPIANS 1:6

> *"Wherefore laying aside all malice, and all guile, and hypocrisies, and envies, and all evil speakings, As newborn babes, desire the sincere milk of the word, that ye may grow thereby: If so be ye have tasted that the Lord is gracious."*—1 PETER 2:1–3

> *"But grow in grace, and in the knowledge of our Lord and Saviour Jesus Christ. To him be glory both now and for ever. Amen."*—2 PETER 3:18

May God truly bless you as you lay down your will, submit to His power, embrace His directives and begin living life His way! You will love living life "different by design"—it truly is the best life, and it truly is a good life!

Questions for Personal Study
Conclusion

1. What does it mean to say that you can discover your uniqueness by conforming to the image of Christ?

2. Of all the principles we've studied, which ones had the greatest impact on you and why?

3. Describe a few ways your life has already changed since you started this study.

4. Of all the principles in this study, which ones do you feel you need to grow in the most?

5. Pray right now and ask the Lord for His grace and power as you desire to have a lifestyle that pleases Him.

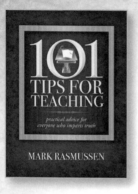
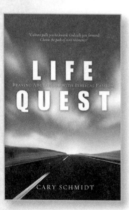

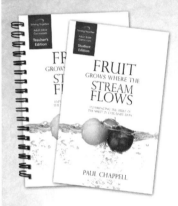

Fruit Grows Where the Stream Flows
Adult Sunday School Curriculum

The only way to truly live the Christian life is to allow the "stream" of the Holy Spirit to flow freely through your life, so He can bear the fruit of spiritual maturity. In this thirteen-lesson study, you will be rejuvenated as you discover what the Holy Spirit wants to produce through you.

Discover Your Destiny
Teen Sunday School Curriculum

Discover what every young adult needs to know about making right choices in a world full of wrong. This seventeen lesson series will equip students to discover the perfect will of God for their lives. The teacher's guide contains lesson outlines, teaching ideas, and Scripture helps.

Jonah: A Whale of a Lesson on Obedience
Adult/Teen Sunday School Curriculum

Dr. John Goetsch brings to life a powerful study in this new Sunday school curriculum. These thirteen lessons will take your students verse by verse through the book of Jonah. This study is perfect for adult Bible classes as well as young adults and teens.

Visit us online

strivingtogether.com

dailyintheword.org

wcbc.edu

lancasterbaptist.org